WJEC
CBAC

C000150348

Coursework Guide

GCSE English/English Literature

Roger Lane

Consultants
Barry Childs
Ken Elliott
Margaret Graham
Jane Hingley
Stuart Sage
Ted Snell

speaking   *Shakespeare*

DRAMA

explore

argue

listening   short stories   *poetry*

OXFORD
UNIVERSITY PRESS

OXFORD
UNIVERSITY PRESS

Great Clarendon Street, Oxford OX2 6DP

Oxford University Press is a department of the University of Oxford.
It furthers the University's objective of excellence in research,
scholarship, and education by publishing worldwide in

Oxford New York

Auckland Bangkok Buenos Aires Cape Town Chennai
Dar es Salaam Delhi Hong Kong Istanbul Karachi Kolkata
Kuala Lumpur Madrid Melbourne Mexico City Mumbai Nairobi
São Paulo Shanghai Taipei Tokyo Toronto

Oxford is a registered trade mark of Oxford University Press
in the UK and in certain other countries

© Roger Lane 2002

The moral rights of the author have been asserted

Database right Oxford University Press (maker)

First published 2002

British Library Cataloguing in Publication Data

Data available

ISBN: 978-0-19-831887-3

10 9 8 7

Printed in United Kingdom by Synergie Basingstoke

Author's acknowledgements

This book is dedicated to Jack Hetherington, almost fifty years a WJEC
examiner and still our inspiration.

Thanks also to Bedwas Comprehensive School, for generous help with
exemplar material; Elizabeth Evans, for research; Stuart Sage and Barry
Childs, coursework supremos both; and Dawn Mearing, for providing
the discerning eye of a practising teacher.

Acknowledgements

The publisher would like to thank the teachers whose
comments have contributed to the development of this
project. They would also like to thank the many students
who have contributed the exemplar GCSE coursework
assignments which are reproduced throughout this Guide.
Each student has been named where their work appears.

Poetry
Lionel Abrahams: 'To Halley's Comet' from *The Writer in
Sand* (Ad Donker, 1988), reprinted by permission of Jonathan
Ball Publishers (Pty) Ltd.
John Clare: 'The Badger' from *Selected Poems and Prose of John
Clare* edited by Eric Robinson and Geoffrey Summerfield
(Oxford University Press, 1967), copyright © Eric Robinson
1967, reprinted by permission of Curtis Brown Group Ltd,
London on behalf of Eric Robinson.
Gillian Clarke: 'Snow on the Mountain' from *Selected Poems*
by Gillian Clarke (Carcanet Press, 1985), copyright © Gillian
Clarke 1985, reprinted by permission of the publisher.
Wendy Cope: 'The Concerned Adolescent' from *Serious
Concerns* (Faber and Faber Ltd, 1992), copyright © Wendy
Cope 1992, reprinted by permission of the publishers.
Peter Finch: 'Some Christmas Haiku' from *Food* (Seren,
2001), copyright © Peter Finch 2001, reprinted by permission
of the publisher.
Molly Holden: 'Stopping Places' from *Selected Poems* (BBC
Worldwide Ltd, 2000), copyright © Alan Holden 2000,
reprinted by permission of Alan Holden.
Philip Larkin: 'The Whitsun Weddings' from *Collected Poems*
(Faber and Faber Ltd, 1988), copyright © The Estate of Philip
Larkin 1988, reprinted by permission of the publishers.
Sheenagh Pugh: 'Toast' from *The Beautiful Lie* (Seren, 2002),
copyright © Sheenagh Pugh 2002, reprinted by permission
of the publisher.

Prose
Bruce Chatwin: Extract from *On the Black Hill* (Jonathan
Cape, 1992), reprinted by permission of The Random House
Group Limited.
Nick Hornby: Extract from *Fever Pitch* by (Victor Gollancz,
1992), copyright © Nick Hornby 1992, reprinted by
permission of PFD on behalf of Nick Hornby.
Lorna Sage: Extract from *Bad Blood* (4th Estate, 2000),
copyright © Lorna Sage 2000, reprinted by permission of
HarperCollins Publishers.

Drama
Laurence Allan: Extract from 'Cradle to the Grave' from
On The Road Again, The Best Years of Our Lives, Cradle To The Grave
(Seren Drama, 2000), copyright © Laurence Allan 2000,
reprinted by permission of the author.
Alan Ayckbourn: Extract from *Confusions* (Heinemann
Educational Publishers, 1977), reprinted by permission of
Methuen Publishing Limited.
Bertolt Brecht: Extract from 'The Caucasian Chalk Circle'
taken from *Brecht Plays 7* (Methuen, 1988), reprinted by
permission of the publisher.
Duncan Bush: Extract from 'Sailing to America', copyright
© Duncan Bush 2000, from *Act 1 Wales* (Seren Drama, 2000),
reprinted by permission of the author.
Arthur Miller: Extract from *The Crucible* (Penguin Classics,
2000), copyright © Arthur Miller 2000, reprinted by
permission of International Creative Management, Inc.
William Russell: Extract from *Educating Rita* (French, 1981),
reprinted by permission of Methuen Publishing Limited.

It has not been possible to trace and contact all copyright
holders of material included before publication. If notified
the publisher undertakes to rectify any errors or omissions
at the earliest opportunity.

Contents

Introduction

This Guide is intended to contribute to the preparation of both English and English Literature coursework in WJEC centres old and new, large and small, in England and in Wales.

The revision of GCSE specifications for first examination in 2004 gives an opportunity for English departments to take stock of the texts they use and the tasks they set. This Coursework Guide provides enterprising choices and inventive ideas to help with this. It is expected that teachers will wish to use some, amend others, and openly reject a few! However, the sections are designed so that a busy teacher can photocopy and use a task sheet or a piece of exemplar material with ease and at minimal cost.

In particular, if you are a teacher taking an English GCSE class for the first time, this Coursework Guide offers, within each section, coursework assignments which can be followed through, step-by-step. Plenty of choice is offered, so that each teacher can create a suitable and challenging course for their own students. The sections within this Coursework Guide provide the following coursework task selections for teachers to choose from:

Speaking and Listening – 9 free-standing tasks, covering individual extended contributions, group work and drama-focused activities;

Poetry – 12 poems, covering pre- and post-1914 poetry, poetry with Welsh relevance and poetry from different cultures and traditions;

Prose – 6 prose texts, covering pre- and post-1914 (including literary non-fiction);

Drama – 8 plays, covering pre-1914 / Shakespeare, post-1914, drama with Welsh relevance and drama from different cultures and traditions;

Open Writing – 4 broad tasks on autobiography, travel writing, narrative fiction, and play-script writing;

Closed Writing – 4 broad tasks on report, formal letter, article and review writing.

Each section has its own contents list, which contains details of all the notes for teachers within that section and the photocopy masters for students. Some of these photocopy masters are general but the majority is specific to the tasks above. The photocopy masters can be worked through as a class to prompt discussion, or distributed to students for independent work.

With so many categories and sub-sets, it is very important that teachers have an overview of the coursework requirements. Opposite, therefore, we provide a summary of the requirements for English coursework (England and Wales assessment options), and English Literature coursework (Specifications A and B). Use it in conjunction with the notes for teachers at the start of each section to inform your planning. On pages 6 and 7 are answers to questions which teachers might possibly ask about the specifications and the course.

ENGLISH COURSEWORK
(WALES ASSESSMENT OPTION)

1. Reading: Welsh relevance
2. Reading: Different cultures and traditions
3. Writing: Narrative/descriptive
4. Writing: Analytical/persuasive

- One Reading piece must be poetry.
- One Reading piece must be drama.
- One piece must be teacher supervised.
- At least one piece must be handwritten.

ENGLISH COURSEWORK
(ENGLAND ASSESSMENT OPTION)

1. Reading: Shakespeare play
2. Reading: Poetry from different cultures and traditions
3. Writing: Narrative/descriptive
4. Writing: Analytical/persuasive

- One piece must be teacher supervised.
- At least one piece must be handwritten.

ENGLISH – SPEAKING AND LISTENING

1. Group discussion and interaction
2. Individual extended contribution
3. Drama-focused activity

ENGLISH LITERATURE COURSEWORK
(SPECIFICATION A)

1. Poetry (pre-1914)
2. Poetry (post-1914)
3. Prose
4. Drama

- Pre- and post-1914 prose and drama must be covered across coursework and the examination.
- At least two assignments must compare texts.
- One piece must be teacher supervised.
- At least one piece must be handwritten.

ENGLISH LITERATURE COURSEWORK
(SPECIFICATION B)

1. Poetry (pre-1914)
2. Prose (pre-1914)
3. Drama
4. Wider Reading

- Pre- and post-1914 drama must be covered across coursework and the examination.
- The WJEC set anthology for Specification B covers post-1914 poetry and prose for the examination.
- Comparison takes place in the examination.
- Wider Reading can be based on poetry, prose or drama, either pre- or post-1914.
- One piece must be teacher supervised.
- At least one piece must be handwritten.

Questions and answers

1. Do Welsh authors count as 'different cultures and traditions'?
Yes, if you are in England. No, if you are in Wales.

2. Can both poetry tasks be comparisons?
Yes. In fact, in English Literature Specification A many teachers will set comparative tasks for both poetry pieces as the most manageable way of meeting the requirements. No poetry comparison is required for English, but you can include one of your literature comparative pieces for convenience.

3. Does the prose have to be a novel or can it be a collection of short stories? If so, is there a minimum number that students should study?
No, it does not have to be a novel. Short stories are acceptable. Students may submit an assignment solely on one short story for English Literature prose coursework. However, it is expected that their reading range will include other short stories for broader experience. The English specification refers to six short stories or one novel as sufficient experience.

4. Can the drama assignment be based on the television performance or does it have to be on the written text?
The written text must feature in the study of drama. This may include plays for film and television. Work based on the viewing of taped or live performances must be linked to study of the written text, for example, assessing the interpretation of aspects of the text.

5. Can the informative/persuasive writing be in any form: letter, report, speech, etc.?
The simple answer is yes. Closed and/or transactional writing features strongly on English Paper 2, so coursework should offer regular opportunities to write in various forms.

6. Are the 'reading' assignments in the language folder marked for reading & understanding or expression skills?
Reading and understanding only. Only when expression seriously gets in the way of communicating understanding does it affect the achievement. Obviously, very able candidates start with an advantage of advanced vocabulary and style, but they too have to show their understanding of the text as priority.

7. Can the same assignment be double-entered for language and literature?
Yes. The two coursework Reading pieces for English can also be entered for English Literature.

8. If pupils study poems that cover pre- and post-1914, can the coursework assignments be entered for any category/folder?
You can enter an assignment that covers poems from more than one category. It can be included in both the English Literature and English folders. However, the same piece cannot be entered more than once in the

same folder. For example, an essay comparing a pre-1914 poem with a post-1914 poem cannot be entered under both categories.

9. Can the Open Writing assignment be autobiographical or does it have to be imaginative?

It can be either autobiographical or imaginative or, of course, like much creative writing, a mixture of both. It can lean either towards the narrative or the descriptive.

10. Will pupils be penalised if the content or subject of their narrative is not suitable?

It is very clearly the teacher's judgement whether or not subject matter is suitable. There are a number of issues that are very difficult for the external moderator to intervene on. Some will be a matter of taste; others will involve issues of verification of the writing as the student's own work. Because coursework runs over a period of maybe eighteen months, teachers have the opportunity to solve dilemmas while the external moderator can only identify the problem and refer it to the board and/or the school for explanation.

11. How far should you help students to redraft their work?

The student should learn to be as independent as possible over the GCSE course. Teachers should not correct every error and then allow students to submit 'perfect' copies in their folder, but obviously they are allowed to teach and advise students how to improve their work. It is suggested that advice written on draft copies should be general. It is helpful to the external moderator if one draft piece of writing is included in each folder, but multiple drafts either on one task or across a whole folder are not necessary.

12. Should students complete pieces for their coursework folder in Year 10 or should they wait until Year 11?

It is extremely sensible for most candidates to begin their coursework at the start of the course and complete as much of it as possible during Year 10. In particular, problems of attendance during Year 11, clashes with requirements in other subjects, and dealing with long literature texts, all point to the good sense of getting on top of the coursework demands as early as possible. Students may replace isolated pieces or fill occasional gaps during Year 11, but they should not return to a completed task and re-vamp the same response. A fresh task on a previously studied text is perfectly valid and the best way forward. Teachers or students who feel that whole folders need rewriting in Year 11 are forgetting that most of the marks in both English and English Literature are earned (or lost!) on the exam papers.

Speaking and Listening

Notes for teachers

Photocopy masters (PCMs)

GENERAL

TASK SHEETS

Notes for teachers

The English specification

Below is a brief summary of the main features of the WJEC English specification and its administration that will change from 2004, as well as those which will remain the same. Full details can be found in the specification itself and/or be obtained from the Board.

Changes from 2004

1. There will be no separate 'oral' grade.
2. There will be no *moderation* videotape.
3. The assessment focus will include 'individual extended contributions' and 'drama-focused activities' as well as 'group discussion and interaction'.

Continuing features from 2004

1. Speaking and Listening will continue to be valued at 20% of the overall English assessment.
2. Advisory visits to schools by WJEC Consultative Moderators will continue on the basis of a three-year rota.

Key terms and categories

Teachers need to be aware of the following terms and categories.

There are three 'contexts' that students should be assessed in for Speaking and Listening work:

- group discussion and interaction
- individual extended contributions
- drama-focused activities.

The contexts above should be cross-referenced with the following 'purposes of talk', often referred to as 'triplets':

- *explain, describe, narrate*
- *explore, analyse, imagine*
- *discuss, argue, persuade.*

It is expected, therefore, that each student should be assessed on (at least) three occasions throughout their course, but the mark (out of 40) at the end of the course should be awarded as a 'best-fit' decision using the general and specific assessment criteria to weigh up strengths against weaknesses.

As always, common sense should prevail in matters of judgement, e.g. a student who has not attempted a drama-focused activity would earn a reduced overall mark at the teacher's discretion. The triplets, in particular, have to be flexibly applied, because it is recognized that to some extent these are arbitrary groupings.

The above categories and terms are used throughout this section, in recognition of the increased emphasis on specific activities, purposes of talk, and oracy skills in the specification.

Organizational good practice

At individual teacher level and at departmental level, the following elements of organizational good practice will contribute to successful outcomes in Speaking and Listening work:

- Some continuity of record-keeping and assessment methods from KS3 to GCSE;
- Self-assessment and/or record-keeping by students (proforma and/or journals) – see section on page 12;
- Informal cross-moderation of students (i.e. teachers exchanging classes for a second opinion);
- Opportunities for pupils from different classes to work together from time to time;
- A semi-formal internal moderation event held annually (supported by senior management);
- Exemplar archive video material of Speaking and Listening activities to be viewed and assessed by students;
- A statistical overview of awarded marks to be shared and reviewed by teachers;
- Rigorous, but sensitive, checks and balances (second opinions) applied to assessment of students with atypical Speaking and Listening profiles;
- A common application of departmental record-keeping policy (agreed by consensus);
- Some common task-setting, but also an expanding bank of successful tasks (a sharing policy);
- The opportunity for an additional teacher to attend an advisory visit for INSET purposes;
- Use of the advisory visit for focusing on an issue of relevance to the department.

Classroom management and assessment

Speaking and Listening activities, especially those involving pairs and group work, require a disciplined classroom environment in order to be successful. Assessment of students, which would appear to be an extra burden for an overstretched teacher, can in fact contribute to the success of an activity – if there is an element of surprise in it (see below).

When group work takes place, no teacher can reliably assess all the students in the class. The most that can be achieved is that a small number of students (around a maximum of six) can be monitored. Those assessed could be randomly selected and discreetly monitored.

There should be **one specific rule** of engagement, beyond the usual classroom code of conduct – **students must not talk to any other students except those with whom they have been selected to work**. This rule should be impressed on all students before and during the task. It should be adhered to, and the teacher should be prepared to act decisively if there is a transgression.

Before the group work starts, the class should be made aware that a random group of students will be assessed formally and given feedback at the end of the lesson. A draw could be made (named or numbered cards), but the six or so selected individuals could not be revealed. Therefore, all

members of the class will know that they are potentially being assessed and are consequently being placed under some pressure to perform.

While the group task proceeds, the teacher should 'police' the class from a respectable distance and not attempt to influence the discussion. The teacher should remain detached, and should only intervene if a significant indiscretion is committed. Privately, the teacher should be observing the selected individuals (who may, of course, be clustered together or scattered in the four corners of the classroom).

At the end of the lesson, the names of the six selected individuals should be announced and a quick assessment of their performances given. These assessments do not need to be technical, but they would be meaningful if, for instance, one student were told that his or her engagement with the task was consistently positive, while another was told that he or she lacked concentration. In practice, most observations of group work from a distance will be about co-operation, though a sixth sense will easily pick up the degree of relevance of the talk.

This approach could become a regular feature of oral work in the classroom. When the procedure is used again, the principle of random selection could again be employed, so that all members of the class are again vulnerable to selection and are, therefore, under pressure to perform.

Self-assessment and record-keeping

In practice, Speaking and Listening will almost certainly be an integrated part of a GCSE English (and English Literature) course. This is both for practical reasons of time management and because students learn through the process of talk. Sometimes, however, Speaking and Listening can become marginalized in an integrated course, remaining out of focus for assessment purposes.

Self-assessment by students is an increasingly popular means of raising awareness of Speaking and Listening skills and issues. Inevitably, it brings the written word into the equation as part of the record-keeping process. Proformas offer a good focus for question and answer and a sense of 'official' policy, but journals too can be highly effective, particularly if kept over a long period. Journals need not be a daily chore but, if used properly (i.e. regularly), they can transfer some of the weight of record-keeping onto the students and can offer more developed opportunities for students to expand on achievement in Speaking and Listening both inside and outside the English classroom. PCM 3 provides a self-assessment sheet for students to fill in. There is also a photocopiable sheet for teachers to fill in for each student at the end of these notes.

Notes on using the photocopy masters (PCMs)

PCMs 1–4 provide general information for students, which can be used at individual teachers' discretion. PCM 1 explains the position of Speaking and Listening within the English course and PCM 2 explains the grading structure and general assessment criteria for students. PCM 3 has already been dealt with in the previous section. PCM 4 provides a sheet of general tips for students on Speaking and Listening techniques. This sheet will be a useful reference tool for students as they work through the remaining PCMs in this section.

PCMs 5–13 provide task sheets for students which cover every combination of 'purposes of talk' (triplets) and 'contexts of assessment'

(see the grid on page 14). They are to a large extent free-standing, although they often link, or can be made to link, directly to other aspects of the course. Their main appeal may be that they can be set up easily, with manageable requirements of paper and time. In these tasks time is a movable feast – it can be expanded or contracted according to other pressures. For this reason, time limits have not been suggested on the task sheets.

- **Personal narratives (PCM 5):** This task parallels the kind of writing that students have to do in Paper 1 and possibly in coursework. If done properly as a Speaking and Listening task, it will raise issues of structure and style that will support students' learning about writing forms.

- **Exploring dislikes – 'Room 101' (PCM 6):** This task, based on the BBC2 television programme, could be introduced with a sample recording of the programme. However, students may find it quite difficult to sustain the arguments and anecdotes that characterize this programme and they will probably need quite a lot of prompting from the teacher. An equivalent exercise for 'Exploring likes' could be based on the radio programme 'Desert Island Discs'.

- **Judging poems (PCM 7):** This task involves small groups of students discussing three poems, photocopies of which have been issued to them by their teacher, and awarding marks under several headings in order to select an overall winner. This task could obviously be linked with poetry study elsewhere in the coursework folder. Similar rules and structure could be used for the judging of media texts or novel openings.

- **Presentation (PCM 8):** This task attempts to give shape to a familiar event, the individual talk, with encouragement to students to think hard about their best choice and the best way of presenting and organizing it. Teachers should be prepared to arrange an alternative venue for the presentation, if requested.

- **Exploring character (PCM 9):** This is an excellent way of placing the onus of literature study in the hands of the students, by asking them to explore a character from one of their set texts and then to present their findings to the class as a whole. This is a presentation, so students should be discouraged from simply reading out essays.

- **Question Time (PCM 10):** Based on the BBC1 television programme, this task involves more students and has more pace and variety than the formal, single-issue debate, though main speakers may have to be prompted with supplementary questions. Discussion ought to be maintained on one question for at least ten minutes, though there should be plenty of questions in reserve in case a discussion dries up quickly. The teacher could issue the main questions to the panel members beforehand, so that they can consider them and prepare their thoughts and opinions coherently.

- **Stepping in (PCM 11):** This task gives structure and context to a simple idea, as students 'enter' one of four poems printed in this file and give an account of the events in the selected poem from the point of view of a character or observer. Written empathy responses to poetry do not convey close understanding of language, but here the emphasis is different – it is the quality of feeling that counts. In this task and those on PCMs 12 and 13, it is important that students remain in role throughout.

- **Job interview (PCM 12):** As elsewhere, this may need the prompting of the teacher, in this case in the role of interviewer, to be successful. However, the context of applying for a seasonal job in a theme park is not an unrealistic one for students to imagine. Searching questions on the personal qualities required for a job in the public eye should be asked by the teacher/interviewer.

- **Opposition (PCM 13):** The roles in this focused debate are quite specific, but the views expressed can stretch far and wide. Give credit to students here who warm to the task of being either a dictator or a hopelessly woolly liberal! Again, either the teacher or a very able student should act as chairperson.

Contexts of assessment and purposes of talk

This grid shows clearly how the task sheets (PCMs 5-13) relate to the different contexts of assessment and purposes of talk in the English specification.

Contexts of assessment *Purposes of talk*	Group discussion and interaction	Individual extended contribution	Drama-focused activity
Explain *Describe* *Narrate*	Personal narratives (PCM 5)	Presentation (PCM 8)	Stepping in (PCM 11)
Explore *Analyse* *Imagine*	Exploring dislikes – 'Room 101' (PCM 6)	Exploring character (PCM 9)	Interview (PCM 12)
Discuss *Argue* *Persuade*	Judging poems (PCM 7)	Question Time (PCM 10)	Opposition (PCM 13)

GCSE English: Speaking and Listening

Record sheet of student performance – variety of tasks

Name . . . . Class . . . . Teacher . . . .

Group discussion and interaction	Comments
☐ *explain, describe, narrate* ☐ *explore, analyse, imagine* ☐ *discuss, argue, persuade* (Tick **one** box as applicable)	
Individual extended contribution	**Comments**
☐ *explain, describe, narrate* ☐ *explore, analyse, imagine* ☐ *discuss, argue, persuade* (Tick **one** box as applicable)	
Drama-focused activity	**Comments**
☐ *explain, describe, narrate* ☐ *explore, analyse, imagine* ☐ *discuss, argue, persuade* (Tick **one** box as applicable)	
General assessment objectives	**Comments**
Participation Communication Understanding	

Vox pop

Below are examples of students' comments on a wide range of Speaking and Listening activities. This page could be used to give ideas for formal presentations, record keeping, and self-assessment.

I'm good at listening, whether it's for learning or for instructions. This is particularly important in my Chemistry and Physics lessons where it may be dangerous to do otherwise...

In my Saturday job, I often have to deal with customers' queries and complaints...

I was captain of the Under-15's cricket team last year...

I have taken part twice in the Youth Speaks Competition. The first time I was the proposer for the motion 'Christmas is a Hoax'. The second time, I opposed the motion 'The World Population Must Be Curbed'...

At school I am regularly asked to run errands for teachers, taking messages or instructions. You have to be prepared for anything when you go into another class!

During a recent parents' evening I dealt with parents by directing them to classrooms. Mr Lloyd had a long list of parents wanting to speak with him so I acted as receptionist by ensuring that parents were not kept waiting, explaining the situation, and alerting Mr Lloyd when parents were kept waiting.

We've got a scheme in school where we help some of Year 7 to read. We started by going up to the juniors last year...

I am a member of the local theatre group. I've had speaking and singing parts in quite a few shows...

In French, every member of the class has to answer questions. These responses are sometimes in French and sometimes in English. Listening is the hardest of the lot...

As part of my GCSE English course, I presented an oral talk on the topic of the Chinese New Year. To organize the oral I made prompt cards that had short phrases to act as a reminder. I tried to vary the oral by incorporating things that involved the other senses, rather than just letting the audience listen all the time. This helped to give the oral more depth and kept the audience interested. I think listening to the two people before me helped: I didn't want my oral to sound rehearsed...

I have taken an active part in group presentation at a workshop in Treforest as part of a business simulation...

I often have to answer the phone at home for my dad's business...

Where Speaking and Listening fits into your course

♣ Speaking and Listening coursework counts for 20% of the overall assessment in English. This means that it is equal in value with written coursework.

♣ Speaking and Listening is at the heart of an integrated course in English (and English Literature). As well as the general grading criteria for Speaking and Listening (outlined for you on PCM 2), there are three general assessment objectives that you must be aware of throughout your course. These are the need to demonstrate participation, communication, and understanding:
1. you have to **participate** in a wide range of tasks
2. you have to **communicate** clearly
3. you will **understand** if you listen and engage.

♣ There are three 'contexts' that you will be assessed in:
1. group discussion and interaction
2. individual extended contribution
3. drama-focused activity.

♣ There are a number of 'purposes of talk' in Speaking and Listening, all of which also relate to either Reading or Writing. These 'purposes of talk' are the reasons why you may be speaking, for example to 'persuade' someone about something or 'imagine' a situation. The English specification groups these 'purposes of talk' into sets of three, or 'triplets':
1. *explain, describe, narrate*
2. *explore, analyse, imagine*
3. *discuss, argue, persuade.*

Making the grade in Speaking and Listening

Below is a summary of the general criteria for Speaking and Listening at different grades. As well as these general criteria, there are also specific detailed criteria which your teacher will be aware of and will use to help with the assessment of your work.

G > F > E

- Students at grade 'E' can speak clearly in different situations and can alter their style. They listen with concentration. They can generally use standard English vocabulary and grammar.
- In individual extended contributions, they try to engage the listeners' interest.
- In group work, they concentrate in discussions and make useful contributions.
- In drama-focused activities, they try to communicate and sustain a straightforward role using speech, movement, and gesture.

E > D > C

- Students at grade 'C' can speak fluently in different situations. They listen closely and sympathetically. They show a competent use of standard English vocabulary and grammar.
- In individual extended contributions, they sustain the interest of their listeners.
- In group work, they participate fully, sustaining their listening and making significant contributions.
- In drama-focused activities, they can develop and sustain a role effectively, holding the interest of the audience.

C > B > A > A*

- Students at grade 'A*' show exceptionally high all-round ability. They listen perceptively to a range of complex speech. They are sensitive and mature in their use of standard English vocabulary and grammar.
- In individual extended contributions, they adapt and communicate complex material in a sophisticated manner.
- In group work, they listen perceptively, making influential and authoritative contributions.
- In drama-focused activities, they can work independently and inventively to create a complex role.

WJEC COURSEWORK GUIDE   *Speaking and Listening*

GCSE English: Speaking and Listening

Record sheet of student performance – variety of tasks

Name . . . . Class . . . . Teacher . . . .

How good do you think you are at talking for the following purposes?
Award yourself a mark out of nine for each purpose. Circle a number (1 is low, 9 is high).

Explaining (making something clear and understandable)	1 2 3 4 5 6 7 8 9
Describing (giving a picture of something)	1 2 3 4 5 6 7 8 9
Narrating (telling a story of an event or experience)	1 2 3 4 5 6 7 8 9
Exploring (investigating closely)	1 2 3 4 5 6 7 8 9
Analysing (examining critically)	1 2 3 4 5 6 7 8 9
Imagining (dreaming up ideas)	1 2 3 4 5 6 7 8 9
Discussing (exchanging opinions in detail)	1 2 3 4 5 6 7 8 9
Arguing (supporting an idea against opposite views)	1 2 3 4 5 6 7 8 9
Persuading (convincing someone through reasoning)	1 2 3 4 5 6 7 8 9

Write about yourself under the following headings, using the prompts to help you:

Participating
(taking part in pairs, and group work, class discussions, drama activities)

Communicating
(speaking clearly, using standard English, planning/preparing oral work)

Understanding
(listening skills, concentration, working out meanings)

Speaking and Listening techniques

Participation	Communication	Understanding
♣ Take a full and active part in all group discussions ♣ Be prepared to give a talk to the class ♣ Be prepared to adopt a role in a drama-focused activity	♣ Put your point across clearly ♣ Use standard English ♣ Structure and organize your talk ♣ Adapt your style to different situations, audiences, and purposes	♣ Listen with concentration to the teacher and fellow students ♣ Support and respect others ♣ Ask relevant questions

TECHNIQUES FOR SPEAKING

- ♣ When you talk to an audience, make sure that your body language is positive. Do not lean or slouch.
- ♣ Establish eye contact with your audience. Do not stare at the floor or out of the window.
- ♣ Vary the tone of your voice; do not speak in a monotone.
- ♣ Do not place your hand over your mouth when speaking.
- ♣ Do not stray from the topic being discussed.
- ♣ Do not repeat points that have already been made, unless you have something new to add.
- ♣ If you are making a short contribution, rehearse it in your mind before saying it aloud. Also, your first sentence of a longer contribution should be clear.
- ♣ Always try to make at least one relevant contribution in a discussion.
- ♣ If you are nervous, try to get a comment in early to 'break the ice' – but be relevant.
- ♣ Do not interrupt other speakers. In discussion, it is a matter of judgement when to intervene. Wait patiently for an opening before making your comment.
- ♣ Always be polite.
- ♣ Be enthusiastic (or at least positive) about the topic or task.

TECHNIQUES FOR LISTENING

- ♣ Always be involved in discussions, even if you are just listening carefully to what is being said.
- ♣ Concentrating will help you make relevant contributions to develop the topic.
- ♣ Do not yawn or look bored.
- ♣ When listening to a speaker, face them and give them your full attention. Consider your body language. You should look as if you are listening. For instance, leaning forward attentively.
- ♣ Encourage nervous speakers by means of the occasional nod and smile.
- ♣ Make notes as you listen; it will aid the discussion at the end.

Personal narratives

Context: group discussion and interaction
Purposes of talk: explain, describe, narrate

Task

Work with a partner, then in a small group, to plan and narrate a personal experience that will interest others.

♣ In pairs, discuss each of the suggestions in the box below. Make brief notes on each item. Each of you should then decide on a memory (covering one or more item on the list) that you can develop into a personal narrative. Your memory could be positive or negative.

> **Try to recall a time when:**
> You helped somebody **OR** you felt inspired **OR** something turned out much better than expected **OR** you achieved something you were very proud of **OR** you felt very nervous **OR** you felt very lonely **OR** you felt out of place and uncomfortable **OR** you were embarrassed **OR** you felt you were unfairly treated **OR** you tried to get your own back on someone.

♣ In turn, plan your stories. You will be expected later to tell the story in a reasonably fluent way to a group of fellow students, so work out the plot and, in particular, an opening line. Decide also how you will finish the story.

'It all started when I went to visit my Uncle Stan. Now he was a big man, and I mean big with a capital B...
*   ...and so I finally managed to creep away without drawing any more attention to myself!'*

♣ It is the role of the partner to ask the questions that will search out the extra detail that is important to the success of the story. The partner should try to suggest ideas to make the telling of the story more interesting or entertaining.

'Add a few more details about Uncle Stan... and sort out the middle bit. Find a better way of explaining what happened immediately after Stan had left...'

♣ Now move from your partner to become part of a group of four to tell your story to a different audience. Each group should nominate one story to be told to the whole class.

IMPORTANT

You may be one of a random selection of students who will be assessed here.

KEY RULE

During the task, do not talk to anyone other than those you are working with.

Exploring dislikes – 'Room 101'

Context: group discussion and interaction
Purposes of talk: explore, analyse, imagine

Work in a small group, then in a larger group, discussing which items should be sent into oblivion – into 'Room 101'.

♣ In a group of three or four students, discuss the items below and decide whether or not each one should be sent for eternity into 'Room 101', the dustbin of history.

> **Would the world be a better place without these things or would we miss having them around?**
> People who make excuses, football crowds, dog owners, whistling, italicized number plates, chewing gum, Marmite jars, Christmas crackers.

♣ In your group, each of you should think of at least one item of your own to send into 'Room 101'. Discuss each item in turn and decide as a group the **ONE** personal item that will get the boot! (You cannot vote for your own choice.)

Guidance: This is meant to be a fairly light-hearted exercise, so try to make personal, imaginative choices. You need to have good reasons for nominating or supporting a particular item, and you have to think of good reasons for arguing against other people's choices. For example, *Christmas crackers* are useless, they are a waste of money, and always disappointing with their cheap plastic gifts and their pathetic jokes... but what would Christmas dinner be without them?

You should avoid choosing something very obvious that everyone would agree with immediately, such as *war* or *poverty*.

Do not nominate individuals in your school, neither staff nor students, for 'Room 101'! Be sensitive to other people's feelings. You may, however, choose public figures who really irritate you!

♣ In a class discussion, try to get your group's choice voted into 'Room 101' by your fellow students.

IMPORTANT

You may be one of a random selection of students who will be assessed here.

KEY RULE

During the task, do not talk to anyone other than those you are working with.

Judging poems

Context: group discussion and interaction
Purposes of talk: discuss, argue, persuade

Task

Work as part of a group, discussing and judging poems.

♦ You should be part of a group that consists of a quarter of the class (six to eight students). Within this larger group, you should work in a sub-group of three or four students. In your sub-group, read and study the three poems allocated to you by your teacher. The poems may come from **one** of these four categories: pre-1914 poetry, post-1914 poetry, poetry from different cultures and traditions, poetry with Welsh relevance.

♦ As a group, consider each of the poems in turn, in relation to each of the following headings:
   1. Content – what the poem is about
   2. Organisation – the way the poem is shaped and developed
   3. Language – the style and vocabulary
   4. Ideas – the messages the poet is trying to put across
   5. Impact – the reaction of the reader; the relevance of the poem.

In your sub-group, award a mark out of five to each poem under each of the headings.

Remember: This is not a direct test of your understanding of poetry. It is a chance for you to show co-operation and teamwork as part of your Speaking and Listening work.

♦ Join up with the other sub-group that is judging the same poems as you. Through discussion, decide which one of the three poems will go forward to the next round.

♦ There are now four poems still in the competition, one representing each category above. Your teacher will circulate copies of the four poems to each sub-group and a similar judging process should begin. On this occasion, however, each sub-group should use its marks for each poem to determine a rank order from fourth to first (4th = 1 point; 3rd = 2 points; 2nd = 3 points; 1st = 4 points).

Note: The poem with the most points overall from all the sub-groups could be displayed (with a brief commentary) somewhere prominent in the department for students in other classes to read. The competition could be repeated, using different poems and different systems of judging.

IMPORTANT

You may be one of a random selection of students who will be assessed here.

KEY RULE

During the task, do not talk to anyone other than those you are working with.

Presentation

Context: individual extended contribution
Purposes of talk: explain, describe, narrate

Task

Give a talk or demonstration to an audience of fellow students and answer questions from the audience.

♣ In consultation with a partner, decide on a topic for your talk and begin to plan it. Assist your partner in his/her choice too. Brainstorm a list of possible choices. You may choose to make a joint presentation, but only if you can make roughly equal contributions to the talk. Even if you choose different topics, you still have an important role to play in the building process of your partner's talk.

♣ Think of ways of interacting with your audience, such as:
  ♣ giving a practical demonstration (e.g. applying make-up to a model or coaching a particular skill)
  ♣ changing the location or seating plan for the presentation (e.g. giving it in the computer room, the gym, or on the sports field).

♣ Make thorough notes in your journal (or on rough paper), then amend them and later transfer short prompts to cards or a small notepad, which you can control more easily during your talk.

♣ Take a 'teaching approach' to your talk, by organizing your lesson plan:
  1. Start by declaring the purpose of your talk.
  2. Briefly go step-by-step through what you hope to achieve in the allotted 5 – 10 minutes.
  3. Cover each step in turn.
  4. Re-cap what you have said (and what else you might have done, if there were time).
  5. Answer any questions from the audience.

Remember the importance of issues such as:
♣ voice (make sure you can be heard easily, don't speak too quickly, be lively)
♣ eye contact (look at the audience, keep changing your angle of sight)
♣ body language (be alert, use gestures)

IMPORTANT

This talk will certainly be assessed as a key part of Speaking and Listening – you may have more than one chance throughout the course, but a strong performance here will strengthen your overall achievement.

KEY RULE

Do not read from a script. (You may, however, have brief notes to refer to.)

Exploring character

Context: individual extended contribution
Purposes of talk: explore, analyse, imagine

Task

Give a talk on the author's presentation of a literary character in a text being studied by your class.

- Research a significant character from a set text. Consider and make notes on some of these topics:
  1. your character's key relationships with other characters
  2. the way your character thinks, speaks, and behaves
  3. what others say about him/her
  4. how the writer/narrator regards the character
  5. the importance of the character to the novel/play as a whole.

Remember: You are not writing an essay. You are preparing a talk to explore a character and share your findings with others.

- You need to show a clear sense of purpose in your talk, so start by mentioning the important things about your character. Talk about the major points and highlight the main developments in or for the character by the end of the text. Make your points clearly.

- Read out one or more relevant extracts from the text to bring the character to life. Explain what is significant about the quotation or extract you have chosen.

- Make contrasts between the behaviour of the character at different points in the plot OR contrast his/her behaviour with that of another character.

- End your talk with a clear message about the character selected and what the author has achieved by creating him or her.

IMPORTANT

This is a Speaking and Listening assessment, not a reading or literature assessment. However, what you say about your character should be relevant, selective, and organized.

KEY RULE

Do not read from a script. (You may, however, have brief notes to refer to.)

Question Time

Context: individual extended contribution
Purposes of talk: discuss, argue, persuade

Task

Take part as a panel member in a version of the television programme 'Question Time', answering questions in a formal debate on topical issues.

- With a partner, make a list of discussion questions on issues of topical interest.

  For example: *Teenage crime – What should the government do to reduce crime committed by young people of school age?   OR: Sport – Do you think that there should be an equal amount of women's sport on television as men's sport?*

  Think of alternative questions on Teenage crime and Sport, and then create questions on some of the following topics: *Bullying, Exam pressures, Parents, Animal rights,* or any other topics on which you have strong feelings. You could also create more speculative questions, such as: *If you were to emigrate, which country would you choose to live in, and why?*

  Write each question neatly on a separate piece of paper. Write your name on each piece of paper. Hand all of the questions to your teacher.

- There should be four or five panel members with another student, or your teacher, acting as chairperson. For each question selected, members of the panel will be asked in turn to state and explain their views. They should try to develop their views at length. They will have a further opportunity to respond to supplementary points and questions from either members of the audience or other members of the panel.

- The chairperson (either the teacher or a student) will control the debate by deciding the order of speakers. After the initial main speeches, members of the audience will need to raise a hand to be given permission by the chairperson to speak. It is vital for the success of the whole debate that everyone accepts the authority of the chairperson.

- When the discussion on a question comes to a natural end, a vote will take place on some aspect of the topic under discussion. A question on a different topic will then begin.

IMPORTANT

If you take part in this task as a panel member, you will probably be assessed for your 'individual extended contribution'. If you are **not** a member of the panel, you may still gain credit generally for your support role in this task in the context of group discussion and interaction.

KEY RULE

Do not interrupt other people. Instead, wait for an appropriate pause in the discusion to make your point.

Stepping in

Context: drama-focused activity
Purposes of talk: explain, describe, narrate

Task

Play the role of a central character or an observer in a poem, who has been a witness to the events that the poem deals with.

- Choose one of these poems, which your teacher will then give you as a photocopy: 'A London Fete', 'The Passionate Shepherd To His Love', 'The Badger', or 'The Whitsun Weddings'.

- Give an interesting and engaging account of the events described in the poem, as if you are telling a friend what you have witnessed.

- Try to create a sense of character and a vivid description of the events you have seen.
  - 'A London Fete' – Find your own words to describe what you have witnessed before, during, and after the hanging.
  - 'The Passionate Shepherd To His Love' – Find your own words to recount your proposal to the one you love **or** imagine you are the passionate shepherd's love and give an account of his proposal.
  - 'The Badger' – Find your own words to give an account of the way the badger has been treated, or imagine you are the badger and give a first-hand account.
  - 'The Whitsun Weddings' – Find your own words to describe your journey on the train.

- Rehearse with a partner, or in small groups of three or four, to prepare for your presentation to the class.

Remember: This is not a direct test of your understanding of the poetry. The main objective is to bring the experience to life with feelings and detail.

IMPORTANT

Your performance in this task will be assessed. However, you may have other opportunities on the course to build on your achievement.

KEY RULE

During the performance, whatever problems may arise, do not break from role if you can possibly avoid doing so.

Interview

Context: drama-focused activity
Purposes of talk: explore, analyse, imagine

Task

You are being interviewed for a part-time job in a theme park.

♣ Imagine you are 18 and have applied for a seasonal job at a theme park.

♣ You will be expected to carry out a range of duties, including:
1. selling tickets
2. dressing up as characters in the park
3. working with children
4. dealing with the public
5. serving in shops and kiosks
6. being part of a team.

♣ Develop your responses in pairs or small groups of three or four. Your teacher will then select three or four students to take part in the interview. Your teacher will adopt the role of interviewer. Students should remain outside the class while waiting to be interviewed.

♣ The remaining class members will be involved in the decision-making process and the debriefing of candidates.

♣ You will be asked the following questions:
1. Why do you think you are suitable for this position?
2. What are your personal qualities?
3. Can you give an example of when you worked well in a team?

♣ Expect further, improvised questions.

Remember: This is a **formal** interview. Try to develop your answers well beyond a word or sentence. You are trying to convince them to hire you.

IMPORTANT

Your performance in this task will be assessed. However, you may have other opportunities on the course to build on your achievement.

KEY RULE

During the performance, whatever problems may arise, do not break from role if you can possibly avoid doing so.

Opposition

Context: drama-focused activity
Purposes of talk: discuss, argue, persuade

Argue a point of view directly against an opponent.

- The class should be divided into six groups and each group should be given one side of one of the following arguments:

    1. A parent who believes in the strict upbringing of children.
    Versus
    A parent who believes in giving freedom of expression to children.

    2. A head teacher who believes in old-fashioned values of discipline and order.
    Versus
    A head teacher who believes in child-centred learning (children making their own decisions).

    3. A boss of a company who creates strict working conditions for his/her employees.
    Versus
    A boss of a company who encourages flexible and independent thinking in his/her employees.

- In your group, prepare an argument for your point of view.

- One member from each of the six groups will then be selected to take part in a discussion on responsibility and independence, related to growing up and the world of work.

- This will be a discussion chaired by your teacher.

Remember: On this occasion your task is to stay in role and emphasize views and ideas that your character would believe in and support.

IMPORTANT

Your performance in this task will be assessed. However, you may have other opportunities on the course to build on your achievement.

KEY RULE

During the performance, whatever problems may arise, do not break from role if you can possibly avoid doing so.

Poetry
Notes for teachers

A range of poetry
Categorizing the poems
       Different cultures and traditions
       Welsh relevance
'Making comparisons'
Planning considerations – organizing Poetry work
       Using the assignment poems and supporting questions
       Using the sample essays
       Explaining the assessment criteria
       General advice for students

Photocopy masters (PCMs)

GENERAL

Notes for teachers

A range of poetry

Students of GCSE English and English Literature are expected to read a range of poetry in preparation for coursework. From the start, teachers and students should regard the choosing of poems for study as a critical part of the coursework process. The study of poetry offers great scope for individual choice of material and personal response on the one hand, and for focused teaching and attention to detail on the other. Students should take an expansive approach to the reading of poetry, but be focused (on one or two poems) for the coursework assignments themselves.

The poems covered in this section are not intended to represent a student's full reading of poetry, merely to offer fresh ideas and extra permutations for study. They have been chosen to shock, amuse, and challenge views on society and personal relationships.

Categorizing the poems

Teachers need to be aware of the four categories of poetry designated in the subject criteria and specifications for GCSE English and English Literature:

- pre-1914;
- post-1914;
- different cultures and traditions;
- Welsh relevance.

Try not to let these categories dominate your planning too much, but monitor carefully the focal poems for coursework essays to ensure that the official requirements are met. It is worth remembering that only one of the two poems normally represented in a comparative task need fulfil the requirement for a given category.

If you feel that it would be appropriate for your students themselves to understand more about the structure of their course and where poetry fits in, a simple summary of this is provided on a photocopy master in this section (PCM 1).

Different cultures and traditions

In poetry (English), this category can be particularly troublesome, as there are plenty of disputed cases of origin and influence. The chosen poems in this unit happen to be African and Asian, but the net can be cast as close or as far from England and Wales as teachers wish. (Students in England can also regard Welsh poetry in English in this category.) If you are in any doubt about your choices, contact the examining board for advice.

Welsh relevance

In Wales, schools follow slightly different National Curriculum Orders from those in England. There is a requirement in Wales that schools cover texts by Welsh writers writing in English or that have a Welsh setting or special relevance to Wales at Key Stage 4 at some point in their courses; many will choose to cover this teaching requirement by following the Wales coursework assessment structure in the English specification.

'Making comparisons'

This is a requirement of English Literature that will affect the coursework balance of those students following Specification A, where 'At least two assignments must show evidence of ability to make comparisons between texts.' (Specification B meets this requirement in the examination, rather than in the coursework.) Comparative study is not required in English coursework, but many students will choose to double-enter a piece of comparative poetry work from the English Literature course as a Reading response in English.

Experience shows that, in most cases, two poems only should be compared. To extend beyond two poems complicates the issue of comparison unnecessarily, and often dilutes the quality of detailed response. There are exceptions, such as the shorter Blake poems in the hands of a strong candidate, but generally this is a line worth following. Make sure, of course, that poems being compared have sufficient elements in common for students to sustain a response.

Structuring a comparative essay is especially difficult for students. Give some time to explaining how to organize a sustained, written response. Discuss issues of coverage, balance, and length. Students will want to know how to start their essay and how to judge when to make comparisons. As is so often the case, teachers need to be skilful to provide guidance, but avoid, as they do so, supplying a template for identikit essay responses! PCMs 9-11 in this section will help with this.

Planning considerations – organizing Poetry work

Using the assignment poems and supporting questions

It is wrong to label poems simplistically as easy, medium or hard, matching them to the abilities of GCSE students at different grades. Teachers have to judge matters much more subtly, sometimes through trial and error, and the raw difficulty of a poem is just one of the factors that has to be considered.

Teachers can legitimately support the needs of their students in setting coursework tasks. English-only (single-entry) candidates do not require poetry comparison tasks, but they may not be able to sustain a response to one poem sufficiently without text-specific advice. It is normally not a large task for a teacher to help students to track a poem methodically.

The use of supporting questions can be adopted (and adapted) for any poem, any task, and any student, but too much support for some students will constrain them and prevent them from fulfilling their potential. Remember, too, that a single-essay response is required in the coursework folder, not a set of numbered, low-tariff answers. Nevertheless, on occasions, supporting questions can usefully prompt even the best students.

A page of supporting prompts, followed by possible essay tasks, is provided for each of the twelve assignment poems in this section (see PCMs 17-40). Students could work, initially, in pairs or small groups before choosing, with teacher guidance, one of the essays for their individual coursework folders. It is important to remember that each student's work, as submitted for assessment, must be individual, so collaboration with other students should be monitored and mediated by the teacher.

In each case, the first essay suggestion concentrates on the single poem, the second offers a comparison with another poem from the set of twelve, while the third encourages a little wider reading and some independent study. All of the tasks are 'traditional' essays in which students should look explicitly at the language of the poem(s). Empathy tasks are **not** recommended for poetry, because they do not normally elicit detailed comments on language.

This poetry section also contains four other poems which can be used by teachers as the basis for work in addition to the task for which they are specifically intended (see PCMs 5, 6, 15, and 16).

Using the sample essays

Highlights from two students' essays are provided in this section, together with comments on them from an experienced examiner (see PCMs 13a and 13b and 14a and 14b). Exemplar material can prove invaluable in the confidence-building and awareness-raising of students. Using edited highlights can prove useful as both a paper-saver and a time-saver. Sample essays are not intended to intimidate students – even the best of responses are inevitably flawed and can provide a point of reference for discussion. They encourage students by showing them what it is possible to achieve, even as a sixteen-year-old. Exemplars help particularly with style. However, do discourage students from producing clones of exemplar essays – by using extracts only or by not permitting them to keep copies of samples. If desired, the examiner's comments on PCMs 13b and 14b could be held back when handing out the sample essays, so that students can evaluate the essays themselves first.

Explaining the assessment criteria

Sharing the assessment criteria with students is again an important step in allowing them to feel in some control of their essay writing process. **Response to poetry** (English – specific criteria) and **making comparisons** (English Literature) are highlighted in this section for obvious reasons, but the general criteria are no less relevant here than elsewhere in the assessment of Reading and English Literature. Sustainable assessments come from common-sense, best-fit judgements, balancing the strengths and weaknesses in a student's work. A basic explanation for students of the grading structure and criteria for poetry is provided on PCM 12.

In the assessment of the understanding of poetry, as elsewhere, the assessment objectives and criteria are similar, though not identical, in English (Reading) and English Literature. Simplifying the grids, lists and grade descriptions, one is left with a loose hierarchy or overlapping set of **reading skills**, as follows:

Knowledge and use of text – location, re-organisation, selection, cross-referencing

Inference and interpretation – reading between the lines

Appreciation of language and structure – the way the writer writes

Connections and comparisons between texts in coursework are, strictly speaking, just a feature of English Literature, but in practice they offer students opportunities to consolidate their other reading skills in English. Many students, however, will not find comparative work easy and could helpfully be steered away from it if they are entered for English only.

General advice for students

A number of general photocopy masters for students are provided in this section (PCMs 1-16). These PCMs can be issued as required to students to give them advice as they read and respond to the poems within this section, and also any other poems which they may work on. A list of these photocopy masters can be found on the contents pages for this section.

These PCMs are not intended to be handed out indiscriminately to students. They should, wherever possible, be mediated by the teacher (for instance, there is a need for the teacher to organize and mediate the task at the bottom of PCM 2). Some of the PCMs will be viewed as less than essential for some students, but they all contain advice and information that may be useful for students to keep for future reference after the lesson.

Where poetry fits into your course

English coursework

♦ If you are following the **England** coursework option, you will need to complete a piece of coursework on *poetry from different cultures and traditions*.

♦ If you are following the **Wales** coursework option, you will need to complete a piece of poetry coursework in the categories of *Welsh relevance* or *different cultures and traditions*.

♦ In English there is no requirement for the comparing and contrasting of poems. This means that a substantial essay on one poem would be sufficient.

English Literature coursework

♦ If you are following the **Specification A** coursework option, you will need to complete a piece of coursework on *pre-1914 poetry* and a further piece on *post-1914 poetry*.

♦ In the **Specification A** coursework option, two of the four pieces of overall coursework must deal with the **comparison** of texts. Poetry offers a good opportunity for comparative study.

♦ If you are following the **Specification B** coursework option, you will need to complete a piece of coursework on *pre-1914 poetry*. There is no requirement for the comparing and contrasting of poems in this part of the course.

English Literature examination

♦ If you are sitting the **Specification A** examination, you will be required to respond to an 'unseen' poem. This is a poem that you are unlikely to have studied previously.

♦ If you are sitting the **Specification B** examination, you will be required to write about poems from the WJEC anthology. This will include a task that requires the comparing and contrasting of poems.

SUMMARY

♦ If you are only studying English, you can write about a single poem for your final assessed piece of coursework.

♦ If you are studying English Literature, you will need to be able to compare two poems. You can double-enter a comparative piece, counting it as the poetry piece for English.

Be positive about poetry

Students are often very uncertain about studying poetry. So, bear the following points in mind as you begin to read more of it:

- ♦ You need to build up your confidence with poetry. Do not worry too much about technical language. Learn to read a poem properly by taking it sentence by sentence.
- ♦ You may not be able to read a poem out loud (in an examination, for example!), but you should try at least to hear the words in your head.
- ♦ See a poem as a piece of drama or a narrative. Just like plays and novels, poems can have characters and stories. Poems may have people, places, events, and twisting plots. Even the shortest poems can have a beginning, a middle, and an end – in other words, they have development, moving forward rather than standing still.
- ♦ Identify the speaking voice (or voices) in any poem that you read.
- ♦ Work out the situation at the start of any poem that you read.
- ♦ Do not always look to your teacher for the 'right' answer – there is often no absolute 'right' answer where poetry is concerned.

Introducing the assignment poems

You will eventually write about only one or two poems in your coursework assignment, but be prepared to read and study several more in the build-up to your essay.

There are twelve assignment poems provided on photocopy sheets, three each in the following categories:

- ♦ pre-1914 poetry;
- ♦ post-1914 poetry;
- ♦ poetry from different cultures and traditions;
- ♦ poetry with Welsh relevance.

They have been chosen to shock, amuse, and challenge views on society and personal relationships. Your personal response will be valued, especially if it is based on a close reading of the text.

The following task will be organized by your teacher, according to the circumstances of the class:

Read slowly, if possible out loud, the poems in each category. Make every effort to control your reading through conscious use of punctuation. This could be done well in pairs, so that there is active discussion of the way the meaning of each poem can be brought out best.

Unlocking the meaning of a poem

What is the content of the poem – what is it about? (For example, is there a 'story'? Are there any characters? Who are they? What is their relationship? What is their background?)

How does the style contribute to your understanding of the poem? How is it written? What words or phrases do you find interesting? How are they organized?

From whose viewpoint are we seeing the poem? The poet's? A character's? How does this affect our reading of the poem?

Each poem will generate its own unique questions to help you understand it, but here is a set of questions that you might ask yourself about *any* poem.

What ideas does the poet want to share with you? What is the theme and how does it develop in the content?

What kind of mood or atmosphere does the poet want to create?

What is your own response to the poem?

Technical matters

You can talk and write about poetry perfectly well without knowing many technical terms. Sometimes, technical language actually gets in the way of what you are trying to say about a poem's meaning. However, sensible use of terminology is a good thing and no-one should feel it is beyond them. Use and increase your technical vocabulary gradually.

Use some of the questions below when talking or writing about poems:

Choice of words and phrases

1. Which words and phrases stand out as particularly important?
2. Which are especially effective or surprising?
3. What are the subtle, suggestive meanings?
4. Which are the words with a strong impact?
5. What images are created by descriptive vocabulary, similes, and metaphors?
6. Are the different senses suggested?
7. Does the vocabulary evoke a mood or atmosphere in the poem?
8. Does the vocabulary create tension or contrasts in the poem?

Sentences, word order, punctuation, and line-arrangements

1. Are there grammatical patterns and features that stand out in the poem? How do they contribute to the meaning of the poem?
2. Are there repetitions, line divisions, or features of punctuation that clarify or confuse the meaning?
3. How complex or simple is the language at different points in the poem?
4. Are there any sound patterns worthy of comment – onomatopoeia, alliteration, assonance, rhythms, rhymes, and stresses?
5. Does the overall shape or structure of the poem add to your understanding of it?
6. How does the whole poem relate to its title or vice-versa?
7. How does the whole poem relate to the voice and the setting at the start of the poem?

DO THIS...

- Always try to make comments that show your understanding of the poem.
- Use the technical terms only if they fit the poem that you are working on, and only if you have a sensible comment to make on the features you have spotted.

DON'T DO THIS...!

This poem contains lots of similes and metaphors. It has an ABABCDCD rhyme scheme... It has six stanzas with four lines in each stanza... There are ten syllables in each line... etc.

Annotation (example)

Annotation simply means making notes on a text. It is a very useful, some would say essential, step in the process of understanding a poem. It is a good collaborative task between two (or more) people, provided one person is not doing all the work!

Here is a poem annotated by two GCSE students. 'The Echoing Green' is from William Blake's *Songs of Innocence* (1789), a collection of apparently idealistic poems about the world.

*Echoing –
lots of shouting?*

The Echoing Green

*Fine weather, beautiful
day. Perfect place to be.
Nature joining in.*

The sun does arise,
And make happy the skies.
The merry bells ring
To welcome the spring.

*Start of day, start
of the summer.*

The skylark and thrush,
The birds of the bush,
Sing louder around,

*Church bells?
Celebrating.*

To the bells' cheerful sound,
While our sports shall be seen
On the echoing green.

*Village green – centre
of the community.
Plenty of noise and action.
Just kids playing?*

Old John with white hair
Does laugh away care,
Sitting under the oak,
Among the old folk.
They laugh at our play,
And soon they all say:

*Everybody knows him
– likes being there
watching. Have their
memories.*

'Such, such were the joys
When we all, girls and boys,
In our youth-time were seen
On the echoing green.'

*The green has always
been there. Heart of
the village.*

Till the little ones weary
No more can be merry;
The sun does descend,
And our sports have an end.
Round the laps of their mothers
Many sisters and brothers,
Like birds in their nest,
Are ready for rest;

*End of the day. Tired,
safe with the family.*

And sport no more seen
On the darkening green.

*Simple language.
Light rhythm – children
playing? People and
natural creatures do
the same. Simple rhyme
also suggests innocence?*

*Darkening – night draws
in. Any wider meaning
suggested? Old age?
All good things come
to an end?*

Annotation (practice)

Now read a contrasting poem by William Blake. 'The Garden of Love' was published in *Songs of Experience* in 1793, four years after the publication of *Songs of Innocence*. In the later volume, Blake was more openly critical of society and in 'The Garden of Love' he attacks the Church as an institution.

Annotate 'The Garden of Love' like the example on PCM 5. Make comments, ask questions and use symbols (arrows, underlining, question marks, etc.).

Make sure the notes are at least partly your own thoughts. Don't rely entirely on your teacher. Make sure, too, that when you write an essay, you make use of all of your notes.

The Garden of Love

I went to the Garden of Love,
And saw what I never had seen:
A chapel was built in the midst,
Where I used to play on the green.

And the gates of this chapel were shut,
And 'Thou shalt not' writ over the door;
So I turned to the Garden of Love,
That so many sweet flowers bore.

And I saw it was filled with graves,
And tomb-stones where flowers should be,
And priests in black gowns were walking their rounds,
And binding with briars my joys and desires.

Biographical details and cultural contexts

Relevant facts about a poet's life are known as biographical details. The cultural context of a poem refers to the general historical period and also the place in which the poet lived, and the influence these had on the poet.

Adding this information to your essay needs to be planned carefully, so the reader knows why you are telling them these facts – i.e. what they add to your understanding of the poem. Here are two general points, using William Blake as an example, which should be remembered when writing a poetry essay:

- ♣ **Link** important facts about the poet and the time in which they lived to the central meaning of the poem or poems. For example, you could show that you know that Blake's social criticism and his own bitter experience are present in the often simple language and striking imagery of his poems. He also wrote during the Romantic period and you can see the Romantic idealism and passion in his poems.

- ♣ **Weave** your comments about the poet and the historical period into your writing – don't bolt them on to the beginning or the end of your essay. (The assignment poems all have very brief introductory comments which will direct you to the key issues.)

DON'T DO THIS ...!

'William Blake was born in 1757. He was an artist as well as a poet. His watercolours and engravings, like his poems, were only fully appreciated after his death in 1827. He was a recluse and an eccentric, but he was also a visionary. He attacked the political establishment of the country, because he hated the injustice in society. He wrote the poem 'Jerusalem', which was set to music and is now a very famous song...'

There is a very clear message for you in this example. **Do not** pad out your essay with biographical details or downloaded information about the cultural context of the poet. Some students mistakenly write pages about the poet and virtually nothing to show they have read and understood the poems. The above essay opening might make you feel better while you are writing it, but it is not relevant.

DO THIS ...

The following short extract, in contrast, shows real understanding of 'The Garden of Love' and its relationship, as one of the *Songs of Experience*, with 'The Echoing Green', one of Blake's *Songs of Innocence*.

'...In 'The Garden of Love', Blake describes his return to a place he once associated with innocence. The happiness once expressed has been violated; the 'green' where he used to play has apparently been built on or at least taken over by the Church. Blake is portraying the Church and its leaders as having imposed control over the lives of the people in the so-called 'garden of love'...'

Writing a coursework essay on poetry

Here is a checklist of tips and warnings:

✔ Your essay needs a good sense of purpose from the start, so include an idea or opinion in the opening paragraph. Don't waste your first paragraph on a polite introduction. Name the poem(s), of course, but say something about them as well. If the task is worded as a direct question, then answer it directly from the start.

✔ Make sure your essay consists of reasonably well-developed paragraphs of fairly even length, typically about three to a page. Make sure your final paragraph – the conclusion – avoids exact repetition of points made previously.

✔ The coverage of your chosen poem(s) needs to be balanced. Don't set out to squeeze every last drop of detail out of every line! Judge how to treat any poem in an even, balanced way – a longer poem will involve more selection of detail, but the way the poem develops and concludes will have to be discussed; a shorter poem will require more densely detailed coverage and perhaps more imaginative thinking.

✔ Your essay should contain detailed references to the poem, including quotations. Quotations should be as short as possible – often a word, frequently a phrase, sometimes a sentence. Do not copy out a chunk of text to make your essay seem longer! Keep the flow of your essay going by quoting and commenting efficiently.

✔ Don't be afraid to have ideas. Write in standard English, but express yourself clearly, trying to explain what the whole poem and its parts mean to you.

✔ If you have two poems to write about, all of the above points about coverage, balance, and length still apply, but you also need a strategy for making comparative points. PCM 9 explains three different approaches to deal with this.

✔ You need to aim for an essay of about 3-5 sides of file paper (average-sized handwriting). Anything much less than 3 sides is likely to be not detailed enough. Anything longer than 5 sides may be long-winded – the best candidates are sharp and selective with their ideas.

As you write your essay, judge its quality against this checklist.

Different approaches to comparing poems

When you have two poems to compare in an essay, try one of these three approaches:

This is a good way of making sure each poem gets treated properly. It may leave you short of comparisons at the end though OR it may lead to lots of repetition.

Approach 1

Paragraph 1
Make some general comments on the similarities and differences between the two poems.

Paragraph 2 onwards
Look at each poem in detail and in turn, dealing with the more complicated one first.

Final paragraphs
Write in detail about the differences and similarities between the two poems, and indicate which you feel is the more successful and why.

This is quite a demanding approach, which may stifle your response.

Approach 2

Start in the same way as Approach 1. Then look at both poems at the same time, comparing them as you go along. For each paragraph, take a particular aspect of comparison, e.g. 'voice' or 'theme' and discuss it in detail.

It is quite difficult to get the balance right between the two poems in this approach. However, it is arguably the best way of making cross-references.

Approach 3

Start in the same way as Approach 1. Then look at one poem in detail. Next look at the second poem, referring back regularly to the first poem, pointing out the similarities and differences.

Conclude with a summing up paragraph and include comments on which poem is the most effective.

Comparing different aspects of poems

You can compare any of the following aspects, but be selective and thoughtful. Choose the aspects that you can develop a little. Don't limit yourself to spotting and listing!

Theme
What aspect of the theme is being considered?

Personal response
Do you think the poet succeeded in doing what he/she set out to do?

Mood
What kind of mood does the poet try to create? Does it change as the poem progresses?

Viewpoint
Is the poem personal or objective? Does the poet view the characters and emotions from a distance or is he/she 'in' the poem and experiencing them?

POEM

Setting
Where is the poem set? Is the setting important?

Narrative
What kind of 'story' does the poet set his/her theme in?

Type
Is the poem a lyric, a narrative, a ballad, a dramatic poem, or a descriptive poem?

Structure
How is the poem put together? Is it a series of arguments, a story, etc.? Is it written in parts? If so, how do they relate to each other?

Style
What kind of images does the poet use? Is the language highly figurative, i.e. are there lots of metaphors and similes? Does the poet use irony? Are there any unexpected twists in the poem? Is the style conversational, complex, formal, or colloquial?

Period
(when the poem was written)
Does the date when the poem was written suggest that there may have been different attitudes then? Does the period when it was written affect the style, imagery, and vocabulary?

Plotting the comparisons

Use the grid below to lay out all of the points of comparison that may be useful for your essay.

SIMILARITIES

POEM . . . . POEM . . . .

DIFFERENCES

POEM . . . . POEM . . . .

Making the grade in poetry coursework

G > F > E

Students need to have a sound general understanding of the poem(s); be reasonably clear about what happens in them; and be able to pick out important details.

In English (response to poetry), students are expected at grade 'E' to show familiarity when describing:

- ♣ the nature of the poem's meaning and ideas;
- ♣ the range and variety of language;
- ♣ the impact on the reader.

In English Literature (making comparisons), students are expected to go beyond straightforward connections of poems. They should begin to develop simpler points of comparison.

E > D > C

Students need to make sensible, detailed responses to the poem(s), referring to the language, the structure, and the themes.

In English (response to poetry), students are expected at grade 'C' to show insight when discussing:

- ♣ the nature of poetry, its implications, and relevance;
- ♣ verse style and structure and tone;
- ♣ the poet's characteristic use of language.

In English Literature (making comparisons), students are expected at grade 'C' to explore connections and comparisons, e.g. of theme and style.

C > B > A > A*

Students need to develop their ideas perceptively and confidently, with subtlety and precision. They must explore and interpret independently and with individuality.

In English (response to poetry), students are expected at grade 'A*' to show originality of analysis and interpretation when evaluating:

- ♣ the moral, philosophical or social significance of poems;
- ♣ the poet's verse, craft and appeal to a reader;
- ♣ the patterns and details of words and images.

In English Literature (making comparisons), students are expected at grade 'A*' to probe and explore subtle points of comparison.

Poetry sample essay (1)

Read and evaluate the following essay by Janina Ratuszny, a GCSE student.

**Compare and contrast the different views of love presented in 'Cousin Kate'
(Christina Rossetti) and 'The Seduction' (Eileen McAuley).**

The poems I am studying are 'Cousin Kate' written by Christina Rossetti in
the nineteenth century and 'The Seduction' written by Eileen McAuley in the
twentieth century. Both poems are based on the idea the narrator has of love.

'Cousin Kate' is about a woman being named as filth after having sex
before marriage. After being 'unpure' the man marries her cousin. 'The
Seduction' tells us of a drunken one night stand leading to a teenage pregnancy.

The themes of all of the poems are based on some form of love.
Although all of the poems have the idea of physical love I believe in 'Cousin
Kate' there is true love. The narrator says 'my love was true, your love was
writ in sand', which basically means Kate's love for the lord will wear off or
wash away. 'The Seduction' is based on a childlike idea of love. Magazines
have influenced the teenage girl's idea of love. The settings of the poems
are different. 'Cousin Kate' is set in a country which is run by a lord that
everyone works for. The lord seems to take advantage of his work force.
'The Seduction' is set in a few different areas. First it is by the docks next
to the 'frightening scum on the water'. Last is in the child's bedroom where
she realizes how 'truly truly frightened' she is.

Most of the language in 'Cousin Kate' is understandable. A few
sentences do not seem to make sense. In 'The Seduction' everything is
understandable because it is a modern poem.

'Cousin Kate' seems to be at a normal pace. Some stanzas have a
quicker pace as we are wondering what will happen next. 'The Seduction'
has a slow pace. This is because of the idea of the title 'The Seduction'
suggesting it's slow and enticing. Both of the poems give us ideas and images.
'Cousin Kate' gives us the idea that Kate is better because she's 'good and
pure' which is repeated later in the stanza. It also gives us an image of the
narrator bragging because she has an heir to the crown. The child is a symbol
of shame but she is very proud of him. 'The Seduction' gives us an image of a
young girl sitting alone. After she has broken her virginity she doesn't feel the
need to preserve anything, so her source of ideas, her magazines, get broken
to pieces. We are scared with her as she is 'truly frightened'. The girl tells us
of how it used to be 'Day trips to Blackpool, jumping all the rides' and now
it is 'to walk through town with a belly huge and ripe'.

In my opinion both of the poems were great. My favourite was Eileen
McAuley's 'The Seduction'. I liked this poem because it is modern. The truth
in the poem made me think of what would happen if I was in that position.
'Cousin Kate' was excellent because it showed the complications in having
pre-marital sex. Both of the poems warned us about what could happen in
those situations. They also show us the techniques poets use to intrigue us.

Poetry sample essay (1) – examiner's comments

The comments below have been written by an examiner to help you evaluate poetry sample essay (1). They will also be useful as you write your own essays.

The student should use longer paragraphs, e.g. by joining the first two together. In the first paragraph, he or she should use some key words that are not in the question. He or she could make a point here about the different attitudes of women and men to love in the poems. 'Filth' needs explaining (it might be too much, too soon) and the student needs to sort out who is 'unpure' and why. Big opportunities to expand the essay are being wasted.

A number of words and ideas could be explored – physical, true, childlike – all kinds of love. There are some good isolated points but there is too much switching about. The student could concentrate on one of the poems for a whole paragraph. The short paragraph says very little, e.g. he or she needs to find something to say about particular details that stand out as different.

Poetry sample essay (1)

Read and evaluate the following essay by Janina Ratuszny, a GCSE student.

Compare and contrast the different views of love presented in 'Cousin Kate' (Christina Rossetti) and 'The Seduction' (Eileen McAuley).

The poems I am studying are 'Cousin Kate' written by Christina Rossetti in the nineteenth century and 'The Seduction' written by Eileen McAuley in the twentieth century. Both poems are based on the idea the narrator has of love.
   'Cousin Kate' is about a woman being named as filth after having sex before marriage. After being 'unpure' the man marries her cousin. 'The Seduction' tells us of a drunken one night stand leading to a teenage pregnancy.
   The themes of all of the poems are based on some form of love. Although all of the poems have the idea of physical love I believe in 'Cousin Kate' there is true love. The narrator says 'my love was true, your love was writ in sand', which basically means Kate's love for the lord will wear off or wash away. 'The Seduction' is based on a childlike idea of love. Magazines have influenced the teenage girl's idea of love. The settings of the poems are different. 'Cousin Kate' is set in a country which is run by a lord that everyone works for. The lord seems to take advantage of his work force. 'The Seduction' is set in a few different areas. First it is by the docks next to the 'frightening scum on the water'. Last is in the child's bedroom where she realizes how 'truly truly frightened' she is.
   Most of the language in 'Cousin Kate' is understandable. A few sentences do not seem to make sense. In 'The Seduction' everything is understandable because it is a modern poem.
   'Cousin Kate' seems to be at a normal pace. Some stanzas have a quicker pace as we are wondering what will happen next. 'The Seduction' has a slow pace. This is because of the idea of the title 'The Seduction' suggesting it's slow and enticing. Both of the poems give us ideas and images. 'Cousin Kate' gives us the idea that Kate is better because she's 'good and pure' which is repeated later in the stanza. It also gives us an image of the narrator bragging because she has an heir to the crown. The child is a symbol of shame but she is very proud of him. 'The Seduction' gives us an image of a young girl sitting alone. After she has broken her virginity she doesn't feel the need to preserve anything, so her source of ideas, her magazines, get broken to pieces. We are scared with her as she is 'truly frightened'. The girl tells us of how it used to be 'Day trips to Blackpool, jumping all the rides' and now it is 'to walk through town with a belly huge and ripe'.
   In my opinion both of the poems were great. My favourite was Eileen McAuley's 'The Seduction'. I liked this poem because it is modern. The truth in the poem made me think of what would happen if I was in that position. 'Cousin Kate' was excellent because it showed the complications in having pre-marital sex. Both of the poems warned us about what could happen in those situations. They also show us the techniques poets use to intrigue us.

There are some quite strong points in the last two paragraphs and a sense that the essay is starting to flow. The student needs to avoid the vague comments, e.g. what kind of 'ideas and images'? He or she should write about what the poems actually have to say. The student needs to pick the details out and have the confidence to say what he or she thinks they may mean. There is plenty more to be said about each of the poems. This work has C grade potential – but the student may need to start again to get the result.

Poetry sample essay (2)

Below are **extracts** from an essay by another GCSE student, Sophie Richards, for the same task as the student who wrote sample essay (1). Read and evaluate them as before.

Compare and contrast the different views of love presented in 'Cousin Kate' (Christina Rossetti) and 'The Seduction' (Eileen McAuley).

The two poets write about the same subject, love, in a similar way even though they are living in different centuries, about a hundred years apart. There is common agreement by the poets that there is an important physical side to love, though it is mainly the men who seek the sexual gratification. The female views in 'The Seduction' and 'Cousin Kate' demonstrate that women favour the emotional side of love and feel that it has more importance. The women in these two poems are hurt and disrespected. Women have their feelings involved and they suffer the implications of the aftermath. In 'The Seduction' we learn that the girl has fallen pregnant 'with a belly huge and ripe', while the narrator in 'Cousin Kate' has also conceived a child, as we discover in the last stanza – 'My fair-haired son, my shame, my pride'.

The common theme throughout the two poems is that the women are reluctant to indulge in sexual activity while the men are most predatory. The title of 'The Seduction' states that the woman has to be seduced. In 'Cousin Kate' the lord 'lured' the narrator, which implies that the girl had to be persuaded. The women gain more satisfaction from the emotional side of love and they want to feel loved. They give in to the male seduction in the hope that their love will be returned. The men selfishly use the vulnerability of the women to satisfy their sexual wants. Evidence of this is in 'The Seduction' as the girl is seduced by the boy and exploited for sex, and he takes no responsibility for the consequences ...

...The beginnings of 'The Seduction' and 'Cousin Kate' differ as Rossetti creates a light atmosphere, using easy-going words such as 'sun', 'air', 'contented' and 'fair'. The language gives the sense of breezy and humble surroundings, and creates an airy and pleasant mood and imagery. It gives the effect that the girl is innocent and naive, and she is happy with what she has got – she has no ambition. In contrast, McAuley graphically describes the Mersey surroundings. It is a harsh environment, and is in an ugly, dirty and busy setting, 'He led her to the quiet bricks of Birkenhead docks'.

McAuley uses realistic vocabulary throughout to create imagery of what ordinary people can identify with. The second stanza coincides with the original impressions of the physical environment of the first, by immediately creating an atmosphere between the two people. Words such as 'darkness', 'creaking', 'spat' and 'fumbled' set the uneasy and edgy mood.

Poetry sample essay (2) — examiner's comments

As before, the comments below have been written by an examiner to help you with your evaluation of poetry sample essay (2).

This is a very confident introductory paragraph. It links the poems securely as it begins to discuss the issues. It plays on the close similarities between the two poems, but comments usefully on the fact that these similar outcomes occur in different times. This looks very promising.

The quality of discussion is quite impressive and the vocabulary of the student is in tune with that of the poets and can match it. The commentary brings with it a strength of feeling and implied condemnation of the men's behaviour that shows real engagement with the poems. It also shows true understanding of the gullibility of the young women.

This final extract shows a committed effort to contrast the language of the two poems. The student shows a willingness to look closely at the details of both poems. They have taken the opportunity to integrate short quotations into the commentary. The individual words quoted are quite well selected and help to reinforce a very clear contrast between the settings. Perhaps the description of words as 'easy-going' is a weak spot ('optimistic' might be better). However, lists of single-word quotations can be limiting and care is needed to avoid assumptions about what individual words can do. The use of a longer quotation must be considered and accurate: the long quotation here does not quite clinch the point about the environment. Comment on such things as verbs and adjectives, should be meaningful.

PCM
14a

Poetry sample essay (2)

Below are **extracts** from an essay by another GCSE student, Sophie Richards, for the same task as the student who wrote sample essay (1). Read and evaluate them as before.

Compare and contrast the different views of love presented in 'Cousin Kate' (Christina Rossetti) and 'The Seduction' (Eileen McAuley).

The two poets write about the same subject, love, in a similar way even though they are living in different centuries, about a hundred years apart. There is common agreement by the poets that there is an important physical side to love, though it is mainly the men who seek the sexual gratification. The female views in 'The Seduction' and 'Cousin Kate' demonstrate that women favour the emotional side of love and feel that it has more importance. The women in these two poems are hurt and disrespected. Women have their feelings involved and they suffer the implications of the aftermath. In 'The Seduction' we learn that the girl has fallen pregnant 'with a belly huge and ripe', while the narrator in 'Cousin Kate' has also conceived a child, as we discover in the last stanza – 'My fair-haired son, my shame, my pride'.

The common theme throughout the two poems is that the women are reluctant to indulge in sexual activity while the men are most predatory. The title of 'The Seduction' states that the woman has to be seduced. In 'Cousin Kate' the lord 'lured' the narrator, which implies that the girl had to be persuaded. The women gain more satisfaction from the emotional side of love and they want to feel loved. They give in to the male seduction in the hope that their love will be returned. The men selfishly use the vulnerability of the women to satisfy their sexual wants. Evidence of this is in 'The Seduction' as the girl is seduced by the boy and exploited for sex, and he takes no responsibility for the consequences ...

...The beginnings of 'The Seduction' and 'Cousin Kate' differ as Rossetti creates a light atmosphere, using easy-going words such as 'sun', 'air', 'contented' and 'fair'. The language gives the sense of breezy and humble surroundings, and creates an airy and pleasant mood and imagery. It gives the effect that the girl is innocent and naive, and she is happy with what she has got – she has no ambition. In contrast, McAuley graphically describes the Mersey surroundings. It is a harsh environment, and is in an ugly, dirty and busy setting, 'He led her to the quiet bricks of Birkenhead docks'.

McAuley uses realistic vocabulary throughout to create imagery of what ordinary people can identify with. The second stanza coincides with the original impressions of the physical environment of the first, by immediately creating an atmosphere between the two people. Words such as 'darkness', 'creaking', 'spat' and 'tumbled' set the uneasy and edgy mood.

This is very promising essay writing, certainly with high-grade qualities. Nevertheless, a lot of judgements need to be made about how much detail and how much personal response to include, how to balance the treatment of the two poems, and how to end the essay.

'Cousin Kate' by Christina Rossetti

I was a cottage maiden
    Hardened by sun and air,
Contented with my cottage mates,
    Not mindful I was fair.
Why did a great lord find me out,
    And praise my flaxen hair?
Why did a great lord find me out
    To fill my heart with care?

He lured me to his palace home –
    Woe's me for joy thereof –
To lead a shameless shameful life,
    His plaything and his love.
He wore me like a silken knot,
    He changed me like a glove;
So now I moan, an unclean thing,
    Who might have been a dove.

O Lady Kate, my cousin Kate,
    You grew more fair than I:
He saw you at your father's gate,
    Chose you, and cast me by.
He watched your steps along the lane,
    Your work among the rye;
He lifted you from mean estate
    To sit with him on high.

Because you were so good and pure
    He bound you with his ring:
The neighbours call you good and pure,
    Call me an outcast thing.
Even so I sit and howl in dust,
    You sit in gold and sing:
Now which of us has tenderer heart?
    You had the stronger wing.

O cousin Kate, my love was true,
    Your love was writ in sand:
If he had fooled not me but you,
    If you stood where I stand,
He'd not have won me with his love
    Nor bought me with his land;
I would have spit into his face
    And not have taken his hand.

Yet I've a gift you have not got,
    And seem not like to get:
For all your clothes and wedding-ring
    I've little doubt you fret.
My fair-haired son, my shame, my pride,
    Cling closer, closer yet:
Your father would give lands for one
    To wear his coronet.

'The Seduction' by Eileen McAuley

After the party, early Sunday morning,
He led her to the quiet bricks of Birkenhead docks.
Far past the silver stream of traffic through the city,
Far from the blind windows of the tower blocks.

He sat down in the darkness, leather jacket creaking
    madly,
He spat into the river, fumbled in a bag.
He handed her the vodka, and she knocked it back
    like water,
She giggled, drunk and nervous, and he muttered
    'little slag'.

She had met him at the party, and he'd danced with
    her all night.
He'd told her about football; Sammy Lee and Ian
    Rush.
She had nodded, quite enchanted, and her eyes were
    wide and bright
As he enthused about the Milk Cup, and the next
    McGuigan fight.

As he brought her more drinks, so she fell in love
With his eyes as blue as iodine.
With the fingers that stroked her neck and thighs
And the kisses that tasted of nicotine.

Then: 'I'll take you to the river where I spend the
    afternoons,
When I should be at school, or eating me dinner.
Where I go, by meself, with me dad's magazines
And a bag filled with shimmering, sweet paint
    thinner.'

So she followed him there, all high white shoes,
All wide blue eyes, and bottles of vodka.
And sat in the dark, her head rolling forward
Towards the frightening scum on the water.

And talked about school, in a disjointed way:
About O levels she'd be sitting in June
She chattered on, and stared at the water,
The Mersey, green as a septic wound.

Then, when he swiftly contrived to kiss her
His kiss was scented by Listerine
And she stifled a giggle, reminded of numerous
Stories from teenage magazines...

When she discovered she was three months gone
She sobbed in the cool, locked darkness of her room
And she ripped up all her My Guy and her Jackie
    photo-comics
Until they were just bright paper, like confetti,
    strewn

On the carpet. And on that day she broke the heels
Of her high white shoes (as she flung them at the
    wall).
And realized, for once, that she was truly truly
    frightened
But more than that, cheated by the promise of it all.

For where, now, was the summer of her sixteenth
    year?
Full of glitzy fashion features, and stories of
    romance?
Where strangers could lead you to bright new
    worlds.
And how would you know, if you never took a
    chance?

Full of glossy horoscopes, and glamour with a
    stammer;
Full of fresh fruit diets - how did she feel betrayed?
Now, with a softly rounded belly, she was sickened
    every morning.
By stupid stupid promises, only tacitly made.

Where were the glossy photographs of summer,
Day trips to Blackpool, jumping all the rides?
And where, now, were the pink smiling faces in the
    picture:
Three girls paddling in the grey and frothy tide?

So she cried that she had missed all the innocence
    around her
And all the parties where you meet the boy next
    door,
Where you walk hand in hand, in an acne'd
    wonderland,
With a glass of lager-shandy, on a carpeted floor.

But, then again, better to be smoking scented drugs
Or festering, invisibly, unemployed.
Better to destroy your life in modern, man-made
    ways
Than to fall into this despicable, feminine void.

Better to starve yourself, like a sick, precocious child
Than to walk through town with a belly huge and
    ripe.
And better, now, to turn away, move away, fade away,
Than to have the neighbours whisper that 'you
    always looked the type'.

Pre-1914 poetry

'The Passionate Shepherd To His Love' by **Christopher Marlowe** (1564–1593) is an Elizabethan pastoral, lyrical love poem, which portrays a common shepherd as an idealistic lover.

The Passionate Shepherd To His Love

Come live with me and be my Love,
And we will all the pleasures prove
That valleys, groves, hills, and fields,
Woods, or steepy mountains yields.

And we will sit upon the rocks
Seeing the shepherds feed their flocks,
By shallow rivers, to whose falls
Melodious birds sing madrigals.

And I will make thee beds of roses
And a thousand fragrant posies,
A cap of flowers, and a kirtle
Embroidered all with leaves of myrtle;

A gown made of the finest wool,
Which from our pretty lambs we pull;
Fair linëd slippers for the cold,
With buckles of the purest gold;

A belt of straw and ivy buds
With coral clasps and amber studs;
And if these pleasures may thee move,
Come live with me and be my Love.

The shepherd swains shall dance and sing
For thy delight each May morning:
If these delights thy mind may move,
Then live with me and be my Love.

USING 'THE PASSIONATE SHEPHERD TO HIS LOVE' BY CHRISTOPHER MARLOWE

To understand this poem, you must explore:

* the character of the shepherd;
* the description of the landscape and lifestyle;
* the possible reactions of the shepherd's loved one;
* your personal response to the sentiments of the shepherd.

Make notes on the following as part of the preparation for an essay involving this poem:

1. How does the shepherd try to persuade the woman to be his love?
2. What kind of life does he promise her?
3. Would she be impressed by his promises?
4. How realistic are his promises?
5. Describe the scene he is setting.
6. What is the effect of using all the images of nature?
7. Explain how the shepherd feels about his love.
8. Would you consider that he is making a proposal of marriage?
9. Which of the five senses does Marlowe use in this poem?
10. How successful is the shepherd likely to be in his persuasion?
11. Find out the meaning of the following words: 'madrigals', 'kirtle', 'myrtle', and 'swains'.

See PCMs 3-5 for further advice on how to explore a poem.

With guidance from your teacher, choose **one** of the following essay questions for your English and/or English Literature folder:

▬ How does Marlowe present love in 'The Passionate Shepherd To His Love'?
▬ Compare and contrast the attitudes to relationships in 'The Passionate Shepherd To His Love' (Marlowe) and 'The Whitsun Weddings' (Larkin).
▬ Compare and contrast 'The Passionate Shepherd To His Love' with **one** of the following poems:
    * 'The Nymph's Reply to the Shepherd' by Sir Walter Raleigh
    * 'Song: The Willing Mistriss' by Aphra Behn
    * 'The Sonne Rising' by John Donne.

See PCMs 7-11 for advice on comparing poems and writing essays.

Pre-1914 poetry

Coventry Patmore (1823-1896) wrote 'A London Fete' in 1890, long after public executions had ceased in Britain. In this poem Patmore objects to the event and its effect on those who watch.

A London Fete

All night fell hammers, shock on shock;
With echoes Newgate's granite clanged:
The scaffold built, at eight o'clock
They brought the man out to be hanged.
Then came from all the people there
A single cry, that shook the air;
Mothers held up their babes to see,
Who spread their hands, and crowed with glee;
Here a girl from her vesture tore
A rag to wave with, and joined the roar;
There a man, with yelling tired,
Stopped, and the culprit's crime inquired;
A sot, below the doomed man dumb,
Bawled his health in the world to come;
These blasphemed and fought for places;
These, half-crushed, with frantic faces,
To windows, where, in freedom sweet,
Others enjoyed the wicked treat.
At last, the show's black crisis pended;
Struggles for better standings ended;
The rabble's lips no longer cursed,
But stood agape with horrid thirst;
Thousands of breasts beat horrid hope;
Thousands of eyeballs, lit with hell,
Burnt one way all, to see the rope
Unslacken as the platform fell.
The rope flew tight; and then the roar
Burst forth afresh; less loud, but more
Confused and affrighting than before.
A few harsh tongues for ever led
The common din, the chaos of noises,
But ear could not catch what they said.
As when the realm of the damned rejoices
At winning a soul to its will,
That clatter and clangour of hateful voices
Sickened and stunned the air, until
The dangling corpse hung straight and still.
The show complete, the pleasure past,
The solid masses loosened fast:
A thief slunk off, with ample spoil,
To ply elsewhere his daily toil;
A baby strung its doll to a stick;
A mother praised the pretty trick;
Two children caught and hanged a cat;
Two friends walked on, in lively chat;
And two, who had disputed places,
Went forth to fight, with murderous faces.

USING 'A LONDON FETE' BY COVENTRY PATMORE

To understand this poem, you must explore:
- ♣ the awfulness of the scene;
- ♣ the behaviour of the people;
- ♣ the attitude of the poet to the event.

Make notes on the following as part of the preparation for an essay involving this poem:

1. Why does the poet begin with a description of the scaffold being built?
2. How does the crowd behave before the hanging?
3. How does the poet build the tension as the hanging takes place?
4. What things happen after the hanging has taken place?
5. Which of the senses does the poet use in this poem?
6. Explain the meaning of the title.
7. What does each of the following phrases suggest?
   - ♣ *'fought for places'*
   - ♣ *'wicked treat'*
   - ♣ *'the show's black crisis pended'*
   - ♣ *'horrid hope'*
   - ♣ *'Thousands of eyeballs, lit with hell'*
8. Find out the meaning of the following words: *'vesture'*, *'sot'*, *'blasphemed'*, *'agape'*, *'Unslacken'*, *'affrighting'*, and *'clangour'*.

See PCMs 3–5 for further advice on how to explore a poem.

With guidance from your teacher, choose **one** of the following essay questions for your English and/or English Literature folder:

▬ How does Patmore persuade his readers in 'A London Fete' that public hangings are wrong?

▬ Compare and contrast the way the poets portray people in 'A London Fete' (Patmore) and 'The Badger' (Clare).

▬ Compare and contrast 'A London Fete' with **one** of the following poems:
- ♣ 'London' by William Blake
- ♣ 'Upon Westminster Bridge' by William Wordsworth
- ♣ 'The Charge of the Light Brigade' by Alfred Lord Tennyson.

See PCMs 7–11 for advice on comparing poems and writing essays.

Pre-1914 poetry

John Clare (1793-1864) was a Northamptonshire farm labourer who wrote nature poetry using local dialect. 'The Badger' might be regarded as a protest poem ahead of its time.

The Badger

The badger grunting on his woodland track
With shaggy hide and sharp nose scrowed with black
Roots in the bushes and the woods and makes
A great hugh burrow in the ferns and brakes
With nose on ground he runs a awkard pace
And anything will beat him in the race
The shepherds dog will run him to his den
Followed and hooted by the dogs and men
The woodman when the hunting comes about
Go round at night to stop the foxes out
And hurrying through the bushes ferns and brakes
Nor sees the many holes the badger makes
And often through the bushes to the chin
Breaks the old holes and tumbles headlong in

When midnight comes a host of dogs and men
Go out and track the badger to his den
And put a sack within the hole and lye
Till the old grunting badger passes bye
He comes and hears they let the strongest loose
The old fox hears the noise and drops the goose
The poacher shoots and hurrys from the cry
And the old hare half wounded buzzes bye
They get a forked stick to bear him down
And clapt the dogs and bore him to the town
And bait him all the day with many dogs
And laugh and shout and fright the scampering hogs
He runs along and bites at all he meets
They shout and hollo down the noisey streets

He turns about to face the loud uproar
And drives the rebels to their very doors
The frequent stone is hurled where ere they go
When badgers fight and every ones a foe
The dogs are clapt and urged to join the fray
The badger turns and drives them all away
Though scarcly half as big dimute and small
He fights with dogs for hours and beats them all
The heavy mastiff savage in the fray
Lies down and licks his feet and turns away
The bull dog knows his match and waxes cold
The badger grins and never leaves his hold
He drives the crowd and follows at their heels
And bites them through the drunkard swears and reels

The frighted women takes the boys away
The blackguard laughs and hurrys on the fray
He tries to reach the woods a awkard race
But sticks and cudgels quickly stop the chace
He turns agen and drives the noisey crowd
And beats the many dogs in noises loud
He drives away and beats them every one
And then they loose them all and set them on
He falls as dead and kicked by boys and men
Then starts and grins and drives the crowd agen
Till kicked and torn and beaten out he lies
And leaves his hold and cackles groans and dies

Some keep a baited badger tame as hog
And tame him till he follows like the dog
They urge him on like dogs and show fair play
He beats and scarcely wounded goes away
Lapt up as if asleep he scorns to fly
And seizes any dog that ventures nigh
Clapt like a dog he never bites the men
But worrys dogs and hurrys to his den
They let him out and turn a harrow down
And there he fights the host of all the town
He licks the patting hand and trys to play
And never trys to bite or run away
And runs away from noise in hollow trees
Burnt by the boys to get a swarm of bees

scrowed = marked
dimute = weakened?

USING 'STOPPING PLACES' BY MOLLY HOLDEN

To understand this poem, you must explore:
- ♣ the way the poet feels towards the countryside;
- ♣ what the poet might be saying about car journeys;
- ♣ the irony of the poem;
- ♣ your personal response to the situation.

Make notes on the following as part of the preparation for an essay involving this poem:

1. What are the reasons for the breaks in the journey to the sea?
2. What kinds of places does the poet stop at?
3. Explain in your own words what happens during these short breaks in the journey.
4. How does the poet suggest the behaviour of the children?
5. How do you think the poet regards the beach, the stately home and the promenade?
6. What is the effect of using *'the rank grass'* and *'the dingy robin'* and the other images in the second part of this poem?
7. What is the meaning of the word *'transient'*? What is its significance?
8. Is there a deeper meaning to this poem? What is it saying about life in general?
9. After studying the poem, how do you explain the title?
10. Summarize the *'rewards of travelling'*, as the poet sees them.
11. What is your reaction to this poem?

See PCMs 3-5 for further advice on how to explore a poem.

With guidance from your teacher, choose **one** of the following essay questions for your English and/or English Literature folder:

▭ How does Holden convey her feelings about travelling in 'Stopping Places'?

▭ Compare and contrast the portrayal of the countryside in 'Stopping Places' (Holden) and 'The Whitsun Weddings' (Larkin).

▭ Compare and contrast 'Stopping Places' with **one** of the following poems:
- ♣ 'Leaving Belfast' by Andrew Motion
- ♣ 'En Route' by Thomas Blackburn
- ♣ 'The Landscape Near an Aerodrome' by Stephen Spender

See PCMs 7-11 for advice on comparing poems and writing essays.

Poetry from different cultures and traditions

Kishwar Naheed is an Asian poet. Her poem 'I Am Not That Woman' has been translated from Urdu.

I Am Not That Woman

I am not that woman
selling you socks and shoes!
Remember me, I am the one you hid
in your walls of stone, while you roamed
free as the breeze, not knowing
that my voice cannot be smothered by stones.

I am the one you crushed
with the weight of custom and tradition
not knowing
that light cannot be hidden in darkness.
Remember me,
I am the one in whose lap
you picked flowers
and planted thorns and embers
not knowing
that chains cannot smother my fragrance.

I am the woman
whom you bought and sold
in the name of my own chastity
not knowing
that I can walk on water
when I am drowning.

I am the one you married off
to get rid of a burden
not knowing
that a nation of captive minds
cannot be free.

I am the commodity you traded in,
my chastity, my motherhood, my loyalty.
Now it is time for me to flower free.
The woman on that poster,
half-naked, selling socks and shoes —
No, no, I am not that woman!

USING 'THE BADGER' BY JOHN CLARE

To understand this poem, you must explore:

♣ the way the badger is described;
♣ the way people behave towards the badger;
♣ the way the poet tells the story;
♣ the poet's attitude to the events of the poem.

Make notes on the following as part of the preparation for an essay involving this poem:

1. What impression do we have of the badger at the beginning of the poem?
2. Track the action of the story step-by-step.
3. How does the poet create noisy excitement in this poem?
4. How does the poet's dialect help the story?
5. Pick out some words that might be dialect words and try to work out what each means.
6. Is the badger presented as an attractive and sympathetic creature?
7. How is the badger caught?
8. How does the poet present people in this poem?
9. How does the mood of the poem change?
10. How does the presentation of the badger change throughout the poem?
11. What is Clare trying to say about badger-baiting?
12. How effective is the ending of the poem?

See PCMs 3-5 for further advice on how to explore a poem.

With guidance from your teacher, choose **one** of the following essay questions for your English and/or English Literature folder:

▭ How does Clare convey his attitude to events in 'The Badger'?
▭ Compare and contrast the way the poets make their protests in 'The Badger' (Clare) and 'A London Fete' (Patmore).
▭ Compare and contrast 'A London Fete' with **one** of the following poems:
    ♣ 'A Case of Murder' by Vernon Scannell
    ♣ 'The Song of the Whale' by Kit Wright
    ♣ 'Bullfight' by Miroslav Holub.

See PCMs 7-11 for advice on comparing poems and writing essays.

Post-1914 poetry

Wendy Cope is a modern poet who thrives on making serious points through comedy, as in 'The Concerned Adolescent'.

The Concerned Adolescent

Our planet spins around the sun
in its oval-shaped orbit
like a moth circling a bright, hot, golden-yellow lightbulb.

Look at this beautiful, lovely
blue and green and white jewel
shining against the dark black sky.
It is doomed.

On another planet somewhere far away in the galaxy
beings are discussing the problems of Earth.
'It is a wonderful world,' says their leader,
'It has roaring oceans filled with many kinds of fishes,
It has green meadows bedecked with white and yellow flowers,
Its trees have twisting roots and fruitful, abundant branches.
But it is doomed.

'The problem with this lovely, beautiful world, you see,
Is the inhabitants, known as HUMAN BEINGS.
Human beings will not live in peace and love
and care for the little helpless creatures who share the planet with them.

They pollute the world, they kill and eat the animals.
Everywhere there is blood and the stench of death.
Human beings make war and hate one another.
They do not understand their young, they reject their ideals,
they make them come home early from the disco.
They are doomed.'

Soon a great explosion, a terrible cloud
will wipe out all the life on this planet,
including those people who do not see how important my poem is.
They are certainly doomed.

USING 'THE CONCERNED ADOLESCENT' BY WENDY COPE

To understand this poem, you must explore:

♣ the role of the 'concerned adolescent' in the poem;
♣ the poet's concern for the environment;
♣ the viewpoint of the aliens;
♣ the heavy irony in the poem.

Make notes on the following as part of the preparation for an essay involving this poem:

1. Explain the simile of the first three lines.
2. How does the poet persuade us to be more concerned?
3. What are the concerns of the poet?
4. What is the effect of describing the earth through aliens' eyes?
5. Why repeat *'doomed'* and place *'HUMAN BEINGS'* in capitals?
6. How are humans portrayed in this poem?
7. Explain the different viewpoints that are evident in the poem.
8. What is the effect of the fifth stanza?
9. Why do you think the poem is called 'The Concerned Adolescent'?
10. How effective is the ending of the poem?

See PCMs 3-5 for further advice on how to explore a poem.

With guidance from your teacher, choose **one** of the following essay questions for your English and/or English Literature folder:

▭ How does Cope use humour to convey her message in 'The Concerned Adolescent'?
▭ Compare and contrast the way the poets use irony and humour in 'The Concerned Adolescent' (Cope) and 'Stopping Places' (Holden).
▭ Compare and contrast 'The Concerned Adolescent' with **one** of the following poems:
  ♣ 'Ballad of the Bread Man' by Charles Causley
  ♣ 'Warning' by Jenny Joseph
  ♣ 'Miss World' by Benjamin Zephaniah.

See PCMs 7-11 for advice on comparing poems and writing essays.

Post-1914 poetry

Philip Larkin (1922-1985) is seen as a social commentator on the behaviour of ordinary people. In 'The Whitsun Weddings', he is observing a succession of weddings as he travels through the country on a train.

The Whitsun Weddings

That Whitsun, I was late getting away:
        Not till about
One-twenty on the sunlit Saturday
Did my three-quarters-empty train pull out,
All windows down, all cushions hot, all sense
Of being in a hurry gone. We ran
Behind the backs of houses, crossed a street
Of blinding windscreens, smelt the fish-dock;
    thence
The river's level drifting breadth began,
Where sky and Lincolnshire and water meet.

All afternoon, through the tall heat that slept
        For miles inland,
A slow and stopping curve southwards we kept.
Wide farms went by, short-shadowed cattle, and
Canals with floatings of industrial froth;
A hothouse flashed uniquely: hedges dipped
And rose: and now and then a smell of grass
Displaced the reek of buttoned carriage-cloth
Until the next town, new and nondescript,
Approached with acres of dismantled cars.

At first, I didn't notice what a noise
        The weddings made
Each station that we stopped at: sun destroys
The interest of what's happening in the shade,
And down the long cool platforms whoops and
    skirls
I took for porters larking with the mails,
And went on reading. Once we started, though,
We passed them, grinning and pomaded, girls
In parodies of fashion, heels and veils,
All posed irresolutely, watching us go,

As if out on the end of an event
        Waving goodbye
To something that survived it. Struck, I leant
More promptly out next time, more curiously,
And saw it all again in different terms:
The fathers with broad belts under their suits
And seamy foreheads; mothers loud and fat;
An uncle shouting smut; and then the perms,
The nylon gloves and jewellery-substitutes,
The lemons, mauves, and olive-ochres that

Marked off the girls unreally from the rest.
        Yes, from cafes
And banquet-halls up yards, and bunting-dressed
Coach-party annexes, the wedding-days
Were coming to an end. All down the line
Fresh couples climbed aboard: the rest stood round;
The last confetti and advice were thrown,
And, as we moved, each face seemed to define
Just what it saw departing: children frowned
At something dull; fathers had never known

Success so huge and wholly farcical;
        The women shared
The secret like a happy funeral;
While girls, gripping their handbags tighter, stared
At a religious wounding. Free at last,
And loaded with the sum of all they saw,
We hurried towards London, shuffling gouts of
    steam.
Now fields were building-plots, and poplars cast
Long shadows over major roads, and for
Some fifty minutes, that in time would seem

Just long enough to settle hats and say
        I nearly died,
A dozen marriages got under way.
They watched the landscape, sitting side by side
– An Odeon went past, a cooling tower,
And someone running up to bowl – and none
Thought of the others they would never meet
Or how their lives would all contain this hour.
I thought of London spread out in the sun,
Its postal districts packed like squares of wheat:

There we were aimed. And as we raced across
        Bright knots of rail
Past standing Pullmans, walls of blackened moss
Came close, and it was nearly done, this frail
Travelling coincidence; and what it held
Stood ready to be loosed with all the power
That being changed can give. We slowed again,
And as the tightened brakes took hold, there
    swelled
A sense of falling, like an arrow-shower
Sent out of sight, somewhere becoming rain.

USING 'THE WHITSUN WEDDINGS' BY PHILIP LARKIN

To understand this poem, you must explore:
- ♣ the character of Larkin, as shown in the poem;
- ♣ the scenes viewed through the window of the train;
- ♣ Larkin's feelings about the places and the people he sees;
- ♣ attitudes to weddings and marriages;
- ♣ the meaning of the ending (the end of the journey, the day, the poem).

Make notes on the following as part of the preparation for an essay involving this poem:

1. Larkin establishes a very precise sense of time and place in the opening two stanzas of this poem. How does he do this?
2. Track closely what Larkin sees in the opening two stanzas as his train journey passes through the landscape of England.
3. In the third stanza he begins to notice the noise of the wedding parties on station platforms. What does he think the noise is at first?
4. What is Larkin's attitude to the girls he observes? How does he convey his attitude?
5. In the fourth stanza, Larkin admits that he begins to take more notice of the people he sees. How does he describe them? How do you react to the way he describes them?
6. Describe what Larkin sees and thinks as the train approaches London.
7. Which details of his whole journey do you find particularly well observed?
8. What would you conclude about Larkin's character and his views on life at the end?
9. Find out the meaning of the following words: *'nondescript'*, *'whoops'*, *'skirls'*, *'pomaded'*, *'parodies'*, *'irresolutely'*, and *'farcical'*.

See PCMs 3-5 for further advice on how to explore a poem.

With guidance from your teacher, choose **one** of the following essay questions for your English and/or English Literature folder:

- ▭ How does Larkin convey his views on marriage in 'The Whitsun Weddings'?
- ▭ Compare and contrast the presentation of marriage in 'The Whitsun Weddings' (Larkin) and 'I Am Not That Woman' (Naheed).
- ▭ Compare and contrast 'The Whitsun Weddings' with **one** of the following poems:
  - ♣ 'A Marriage' by R. S. Thomas
  - ♣ 'Bookends' by Tony Harrison
  - ♣ 'Her Husband' by Ted Hughes.

See PCMs 7-11 for advice on comparing poems and writing essays.

Post-1914 poetry

Molly Holden (1927-1981) is a lesser-known English poet of the twentieth century. In 'Stopping Places' she explores the idea that the details of a journey are more memorable than the destination.

Stopping Places

The long car journeys to the sea
must have their breaks, not always
in towns where there's no room
to park but at the pavement's edge,
in villages, or by the woods, or in lay-bys
vibrating to the passage of fast cars.
The seat's pushed forward, the boot's lifted,
the greaseproof paper
rustles encouragingly. The children
climb to the ground and posture about,
talk, clamber on gates, eat noisily.
They're herded back, the journey
continues.
                        What do you think
they'll remember most of that holiday?
the beach? the stately home?
the hot kerb of the promenade?
No. It will often be those nameless places
where they stopped, perhaps for no more
than minutes. The rank grass
and the dingy robin by the overflowing
bin for waste, the gravel ridged by
numerous wheels and the briared wood
that no one else had bothered
to explore, the long inviting field
down which there wasn't time
to go – these will stick in their memories
when beauty spots evaporate.
Was it worth the expense?
                        but
these are the rewards of travelling.
There must be an end in sight
for the transient stopping places
to be necessary, to be memorable.

USING 'I AM NOT THAT WOMAN' BY KISHWAR NAHEED

To understand this poem, you must explore:

- ♣ the situation of the woman in the poem;
- ♣ the strength of her appeal;
- ♣ the oppression of women by men;
- ♣ your personal response to the sentiments, ideas, and language of the poem.

Make notes on the following as part of the preparation for an essay involving this poem:

1. What is the effect of '*I am*' being repeated at the start of each stanza?
2. Who do you think the woman is speaking to?
3. Describe the character of the woman.
4. What is the effect of each of these images?
   - ♣ *'my voice cannot be smothered by stones'*
   - ♣ *'crushed / with the weight of custom and tradition'*
   - ♣ *'chains cannot smother my fragrance'*
   - ♣ *'get rid of a burden'*
   - ♣ *'the commodity you traded in'*
5. Why do you think the poet repeats the word '*chastity*'?
6. Explain in your own words the meaning of the title 'I Am Not That Woman'.
7. Does the poem fill the reader with a sense of hope or hopelessness?

See PCMs 3-5 for further advice on how to explore a poem.

Task

With guidance from your teacher, choose **one** of the following essay questions for your English and/or English Literature folder:

- ▬ How does Naheed express her objections to the way the woman has been treated in 'I Am Not That Woman'?
- ▬ Compare and contrast the presentation of marriage in 'I Am Not That Woman' (Naheed) and 'The Whitsun Weddings' (Larkin).
- ▬ Compare and contrast 'I Am Not That Woman' with **one** of the following poems:
  - ♣ 'Woman Work' by Maya Angelou
  - ♣ 'Maiden Name' by Philip Larkin
  - ♣ 'Choices' by Liz Lochhead.

See PCMs 7-11 for advice on comparing poems and writing essays.

Poetry from different cultures and traditions

Seitlhamo Motsapi is a South African poet who writes in his poem 'andif' [and if] about the struggle of black people for human rights.

andif

it is that time
it is that time love
the moon finally speaks with her six tongues
the rivers now forget the ocean
the mountain finally spits us out
from her centuries old sanctuary

it's the time of traitors
hasty like alligators in search of graves
it's the time of the long machete
arrogant like storms that blow into hearts
it's the time of nights
clamorous like abysses where death rests
it's that time my love
the mountain floods us her angry weals
that bruise screams into whispers

i want you only to remember
the lacerated earth that bleeds into your feet
i want you only to remember
the past that screams at us
from the rent bellies of weary skies
the multiple incisions of dead loves
hurry our hearts into skewed postures

tomorrow there'll be no chain or chafe
no bleed or slit – no gash or ash
to whirl us into genocidal frenzies
there'll be no coffins with incomplete crosses
for men who died without crowns or rainbows
there'll be no knee dancing into a bruise

the lungs of dungeons will suddenly burst
into breezes that remember our wounds

there'll be only you & me
& vengeant warriors with spears knotted
into rainbows
there'll be me & you only
& our hearts mad with insistent loves
that demand mountains & skies
    skies & suns!
    the ancient composure of the hills!
    the roar of rains for all of us!
    the obstinate roar rage of the ocean
    for all of us!
    the eternal holler of hope
    for all of us!

the sprout of dreams & hymns
    for all of us

without delay!

USING 'ANDIF' BY SEITLHAMO MOTSAPI

To understand this poem, you must explore:

♠ the violence in the past and present in South Africa and the hope for peace in the future;
♠ the personal relationship that runs through the poem;
♠ the images of nature and conflict.

Make notes on the following as part of the preparation for an essay involving this poem:

1. How does the poet describe the way life has been and the way life is for his people?
2. What do you think is suggested by *'it is that time'*?
3. What do you think is suggested by *'it's the time of traitors...it's the time of nights'*?
4. Explain what is suggested by each of the following images:
♠ *'lacerated earth'*
♠ *'multiple incisions'*
♠ *'genocidal frenzies'*.
5. What do you think the following two lines mean?
♠ *'the lungs of dungeons will suddenly burst into breezes that remember our wounds'*
6. How does the mood of the poem change?
7. In what way is it possible to call this a love poem?
8. Does the poem fill the reader with a sense of hope or a sense of hopelessness?
9. What do you think the title 'andif' [and if] suggests?

See PCMs 3-5 for further advice on how to explore a poem.

With guidance from your teacher, choose **one** of the following essay questions for your English and/or English Literature folder:

▭ How does Motsapi convey black people's struggle for human rights in 'andif'?
▭ Compare and contrast the presentation of oppression in 'andif' (Motsapi) and 'I Am Not That Woman' (Naheed).
▭ Compare and contrast 'andif' with **one** of the following poems:
♠ 'Hurting World' by Benjamin Zephaniah
♠ 'Still I Rise' by Maya Angelou
♠ 'The Chimney Sweep' by William Blake.

See PCMs 7-11 for advice on comparing poems and writing essays.

Poetry from different cultures and traditions

Lionel Abrahams is a South African poet whose poem 'To Halley's Comet' looks away from his place on earth towards the stars.

To Halley's Comet

Good evening, little visitor.
We know you're there, it's in the news.
But who'd have thought you'd be so shy,
so hard to spot, among the stars?
Who'd have thought, instead of streaking through,
flashing that famous double tail,
autographing the prophetic sky,
you'd do an elusive Garbo act?
Perhaps it's because, this time round
you find we know too much
about a dirty undense snowball
only as big as Table Mountain, say,
that only shines because the sun
lends it a bit of common light.
You've lost your ancient awesome mysteries
your sign-dimension that could move
the old Wise Men, King Harold and Mark Twain.
And so you shrink and hide among our city lights,
claiming a different subtlety.
I like it, in a way: it's less fun
but somehow more moving, that after all
you're so minute and fragile:
you enter our domestic patch of sky
not barging heavy like some line steamer,
sky-bus or iron-railed train,
but lightly, chancily, only just making
your long, lonely orbit
by the skin of your momentum.
We should applaud like mad
that you make it again on time.
You've shed the scary Nostradamus mask
and now drop by, like some private rare Aunt Maud
between prodigious travels,
merely to show yourself and check our face.
No more the fortune-teller, dearest Aunt,
by never getting lost along
those shifting paths of lonely space,
arriving as expected after a lifetime's lapse,
you give us your gift, allow that we
achieve a stroke of prophecy.
We thank you, little comforter:
the dark potent emptiness ahead
contains one probable smear of light.

WJEC COURSEWORK GUIDE **Poetry**

USING 'TO HALLEY'S COMET' BY LIONEL ABRAHAMS

To understand this poem, you must explore:
- ♣ details about Halley's Comet and why it fascinates the poet;
- ♣ what has changed since ancient times;
- ♣ how humankind still looks for meaning;
- ♣ the poet's interest in the passing of time;
- ♣ the character and imagination of the poet.

Make notes on the following as part of the preparation for an essay involving this poem:

1. Describe the latest arrival of Halley's Comet at the start of the poem.
2. How does the poet make us feel so affectionate towards Halley's Comet?
3. Why mention '*Table Mountain*' and, later, '*our domestic patch of sky*'?
4. Why is the poet comforted by the latest appearance of Halley's Comet?
5. What is the effect of using the names of famous people?
6. How has humankind's relationship with Halley's Comet changed?
7. What is the significance of mentioning Nostradamus?
8. What meaning is being expressed about Halley's Comet at the end of the poem?
9. What do you think the arrival of Halley's Comet has done for the poet?
10. Find out the meanings of the following words: '*prophetic*', '*prodigious*', and '*potent*'.

See PCMs 3-5 for further advice on how to explore a poem.

With guidance from your teacher, choose **one** of the following essay questions for your English and/or English Literature folder:

▭ How does Abrahams develop his attitude towards the comet in 'To Halley's Comet'?

▭ Compare and contrast the general view of the world as presented in 'To Halley's Comet' (Abrahams) and 'The Concerned Adolescent' (Cope).

▭ Compare and contrast 'To Halley's Comet' with **one** of the following poems:
- ♣ '299,792.5 Kilometres a Second' by Nigel Jenkins
- ♣ 'Accidents of Birth' by William Meredith
- ♣ 'Bermudas' by Andrew Marvell.

See PCMs 7-11 for advice on comparing poems and writing essays.

Poetry with Welsh relevance

Sheenagh Pugh is a Welsh poet with a strong sense of irony. 'Toast' is set in Cardiff and recalls the summer of 1999 and the building in the city of the Millennium Stadium.

Toast

When I'm old, I'll say *the summer*
they built the stadium. And I won't mean

the council. I'll be hugging the memory
of how, open to sun and the judgement

of passing eyes, young builders lay
golden and melting on hot pavements,

the toast of Cardiff. Each blessed lunchtime
Westgate Street, St. John's, the Hayes

were lined with fit bodies; forget
the jokes, these jeans were fuzz stretched tight

over unripe peaches. Sex objects,
and happily up for it. When women

sauntered by, whistling, they'd bask
in warm smiles, browning slowly, loving

the light. Sometimes they'd clock men
looking them over. It made no odds;

they never got mad; it was too heady
being young and fancied and in the sun.

They're gone now; all we have left of them
this vast concrete-and-glass mother-ship

that seems to have landed awkwardly
in our midst. And Westgate's dark

with November rain, but different, as if
the stones retain heat, secret impressions

of shoulder-blades, shallow cups,
as sand would do. The grey façade

of the empty auction house, three storeys
of boarded windows, doesn't look sad,

more like it's closed its eyes, breathing in
the smell of sweat, sunblock, confidence.

USING 'TOAST' BY SHEENAGH PUGH

To understand this poem, you must explore:
- the sense of place and time;
- the sense of fun and self-confidence;
- the idea of stereotypes and role-reversal;
- the building of the Millennium Stadium;
- your personal response to the images of Cardiff and Wales.

Make notes on the following as part of the preparation for an essay involving this poem:

1. How does the poet give an impression of summer?
2. Why do you think the men are *'the toast of Cardiff'*?
3. What is the effect of listing *'Westgate Street, St John's, the Hayes'*?
4. What is the effect of the words *'When women / sauntered by, whistling'*?
5. How would you describe the voice of the poet, narrating these summer memories?
6. What is your personal response to the lunchtime scene, as described?
7. What impression is given of the Millennium Stadium when finished?
8. What is the significance of *'as if / the stones retain heat'* and *'doesn't look sad'*?
9. Why is the Millennium Stadium mentioned so little in the poem?
10. Why do you think the poem is entitled 'Toast'?
11. Are the images of Cardiff and Wales positive in this poem?

See PCMs 3-5 for further advice on how to explore a poem.

With guidance from your teacher, choose one of the following essay questions for your English and/or English Literature folder:

- How does Pugh portray Cardiff and its people in 'Toast'?
- Compare and contrast the portrayal of Wales in 'Toast' (Pugh) and 'Some Christmas Haiku' (Finch).
- Compare and contrast 'Toast' with one of the following poems:
  - 'Welsh Landscape' by R. S. Thomas
  - 'I Hear America Singing' by Walt Whitman
  - 'Home Thoughts, From Abroad' by Robert Browning.

See PCMs 7-11 for advice on comparing poems and writing essays.

Poetry with Welsh relevance

Peter Finch is a Welsh poet with sharp wit, whose poem 'Some Christmas Haiku' presents readers with challenging views and imagery of Wales.

Some Christmas Haiku

On the moors
The snow caught by grass
No one to see it

Not Christmas holy silent night
But the holiday season
Above the cloud the same old moon

Cinio Nadolig
boldly praising Iesu
Menu's in English

In the chapel
Old wood
After so many years still shining

Through the dense firs
Light of a wrecked car
Burning

Outside the building society
A man in a Santa suit
And three women smoking

Nadolig heddwch
half of Wales don't care
Other half can't pronounce it

Sound of retching
Three men in an empty street
Crushing lager cans

Nadolig sale sign shop closes
can't wait
for it to open again

Sod dolig this bunt
mmm do it dunit
don matter do it again

USING 'SOME CHRISTMAS HAIKU' BY PETER FINCH

To understand this poem, you must explore:

♠ the poet's challenging sense of humour;
♠ the range of images of Wales;
♠ the poet's attitude to Christmas;
♠ your personal response to these snapshots of Wales.

Make notes on the following as part of the preparation for an essay involving this poem:

1. Does the poem start with a positive, natural, Christmas card image of Wales?
2. What does the second haiku say about modern Christmas?
3. What point is being made about language in the third haiku?
4. What comment is being made about religion in the fourth haiku?
5. Why include such a non-Christmas image in the fifth haiku?
6. What is the significance of the street scene in the sixth haiku?
7. What is your personal response to the opinion expressed in the seventh haiku?
8. What is your response to the image in the eighth haiku?
9. Is there a moral to be drawn from the idea expressed in the ninth haiku?
10. What is the effect of the final haiku as a closing statement on Christmas?
11. How effective is the collection of haiku in sketching a picture of Wales at Christmas?
12. What is your personal response to the poet's attempt to shock and amuse?

See PCMs 3-5 for further advice on how to explore a poem.

With guidance from your teacher, choose **one** of the following essay questions for your English and/or English Literature folder:

▭ How does Finch portray Wales at Christmas in 'Some Christmas Haiku'?
▭ Compare and contrast the images of Wales in 'Some Christmas Haiku' (Finch) and 'Snow on the Mountain' (Clarke).
▭ Compare and contrast 'Some Christmas Haiku' with **one** of the following poems:
   ♠ 'Innocent's Song' by Charles Causley
   ♠ 'Christmas' by John Clare
   ♠ 'A Star in the East' by Idris Davies.

See PCMs 7-11 for advice on comparing poems and writing essays.

Poetry with Welsh relevance

Gillian Clarke is a Welsh poet with a strong sense of the nature and history of her country. These are present in her poem 'Snow on the Mountain', which describes a particular incident.

Snow on the Mountain

There was a girl riding a white pony
Which seemed an elemental part
Of the snow. A crow cut a clean line
Across the hill, which we grasped as a rope
To pull us up the pale diagonal.

The point was to be first at the top
Of the mountain. Our laughter bounced far
Below us like five fists full of pebbles. About us
Lay the snow, deep in the hollows,
Very clean and dry, untouched.

I arrived breathless, my head breaking
The surface of the glittering light, thinking
No place could claim more beauty, white
Slag tips like cones of sugar spun
By the pit wheels under Machen mountain.

I sat on a rock in the sun, watching
My snowboys play. Pit villages shine
Like anthracite. Completed, the pale rider
Rode away. I turned to him and saw
His joy fall like the laughter down a dark
Crack. The black crow shadowed him.

USING 'SNOW ON THE MOUNTAIN' BY GILLIAN CLARKE

To understand this poem, you must explore:

* the sense of nature and history of Wales;
* the sense of mystery;
* the descriptive and narrative qualities of the poet.

Make notes on these questions as part of the preparation for an essay involving this poem:

1. What is your response to the first sentence of the poem?
2. What things are clear about the walk to the top of the mountain?
3. What effect does the snow have on the people and the countryside?
4. Why does the poet combine images of nature and industry?
5. Why perhaps does the focus change from '*we*' to '*I*' in the second half of the poem?
6. What is the significance of '*anthracite*'?
7. Can you attempt to explain the sentence '*Completed, the pale rider / Rode away*'?
8. Who might '*My snowboys*' and '*him*' be in the last stanza of the poem?
9. What do you think happens at or near the end of the poem?
10. What is the significance of the last sentence of the poem?
11. Is the sense of history in the poem a positive feature or a burden?
12. What do you think the poem is about?

See PCMs 3-5 for further advice on how to explore a poem.

With guidance from your teacher, choose **one** of the following essay questions for your English and/or English Literature folder:

▬ How does Clarke create a sense of mystery in 'Snow on the Mountain'?
▬ Compare and contrast the poets' portrayal of images of Wales in 'Snow on the Mountain' (Clarke) and 'Toast' (Pugh).
▬ Compare and contrast 'Snow on the Mountain' with **one** of the following poems:
  * 'Stopping by Woods on a Snowy Evening' by Robert Frost
  * 'Mid-term Break' by Seamus Heaney
  * 'June 1966' by Gavin Ewart.

See PCMs 7-11 for advice on comparing poems and writing essays.

Prose

Notes for teachers

A range of prose
Categorizing the prose
Planning considerations – organizing work on prose
       Notes on using the photocopy masters (PCMs)
       Empathy tasks
       The texts covered in this section

Photocopy masters (PCMs)

Notes for teachers

A range of prose

Prose is likely to form the backbone of students' reading during their GCSE English course. There are some important distinctions to be made between English and English Literature, between written examination and coursework, and, not least, between statutory assessment and specification content. Acknowledging the importance of prose in the development of students' language, teachers are expected to provide the following range of Reading for GCSE English:

- At least one novel or six short stories of sufficient length to show development in plot, character, style and related aspects, in preparation for the Paper 1 Reading task.

The overall range of Reading (including poetry and drama) must include texts of Welsh relevance (in the Wales assessment option) and work by a major writer from the English literary heritage.

English Reading coverage, through classwork and homework, over the one or two years of the course, should ensure that all students gain the appropriate experience. Students following the GCSE English Literature course will meet the requirements of the subject through the completion of coursework tasks and study for the examination.

An enlightened and organized approach to a range of prose reading will contribute significantly to students' levels of achievement by helping them to:

- prepare for the reading and understanding demands of a prose passage from the English literary heritage in English Paper 1;
- develop skills in Open Writing for both coursework and English Paper 1;
- prepare for the prose section of the English Literature examination (Specification A or B);
- develop skills for English Literature prose coursework.

Categorizing the prose

Teachers need to be aware of the two categories of prose designated in the criteria and specifications for GCSE English Literature:

- pre-1914 prose
- post-1914 prose

In English Literature Specification A, teachers should make their choice of prose text(s) for coursework study with full awareness of their intended choice for the examination. The final assessed work (for both coursework and examination) must include texts published before and after 1914.

In English Literature Specification B, teachers must select for coursework study a pre-1914 prose text of some substance (or a number of shorter texts by the same author). The requirement to study post-1914 prose will be covered in the examination by the short-story material in the WJEC anthology. The Wider Reading coursework requirement in Specification B may be covered by any genre, either pre- or post-1914.

The prose English Literature coursework assignment may be based on the reading of literary non-fiction, as long as the pre/post-1914 balance is maintained.

Planning considerations – organizing work on prose

Notes on using the photocopy masters (PCMs)

PCMs 1-7 provide general information for students, which can be used at an individual teacher's discretion. PCM 1 explains the position of prose within the English and English Literature courses, and PCM 2 explains the grading structure and relevant assessment criteria for students, focussing on the English (response to prose) and English Literature (making comparisons) criteria. PCM 3 provides general guidance when reading and responding to any prose text, and will be a useful reference tool for students when they begin work on the task sheets. Similarly, PCM 4 will be a useful reference and checklist as students begin to draft out their own coursework essays. This checklist is followed by extracts from a sample student essay (PCM 5), which can be used as a practical discussion exercise about good and bad points before students begin their own work.

Empathy tasks

PCMs 6 and 7 concern the issue of empathy tasks. Teachers need to be aware of the task-setting and assessment issues that are raised by this kind of response to literature. Empathy tasks can work well, but they need to be set thoughtfully and assessed rigorously. PCM 6 provides general guidance for students about empathy work – what it is and how they should go about it. PCM 7 provides a student example for evaluation and discussion.

The texts covered in this section

There are six texts covered in this section (on PCMs 8-19). There are three each in the pre- and post-1914 categories. Texts that have been widely used in coursework in recent years have been omitted in favour of choices that might strike a chord with teachers wishing to try something new. The prescribed list of examination texts for English Literature Specification A is also ignored in this section, even though the texts can be used for coursework tasks, provided sufficient texts are studied overall and there is no duplication of study for the examination.

The task sheet for each text is preceded by a PCM with an extract from the text concerned. Each task sheet contains a number of supporting prompt questions to ensure that the student has a thorough knowledge of the text as a whole before beginning their essay task proper. Two main tasks then follow, for students to choose from with guidance from their teacher. The first task option in each case makes use of the extract on the preceding PCM as a framework and then broadens out to deal with the text as a whole. The second task option is a self-standing examination of one aspect of the complete text. Teachers can, obviously, adapt these tasks if so desired, or add additional options of their own.

Where prose fits into your course

What is prose? Prose is ordinary written English (not drama or poetry). In GCSE English, it includes novels, short stories, and autobiographies. It can be both fiction and non-fiction.

English coursework

♦ **Reading:** no study of prose is required in this section of the coursework.

♦ **Writing:** the experience of reading and studying prose extracts and whole texts will greatly benefit you in the areas of writing to *explore, imagine, entertain* and writing to *inform, explain, describe.*

English examinations

♦ **In Paper 1 Section A**, your understanding of a prose extract by a major writer will be tested.

♦ **In Paper 1 Section B**, your descriptive and narrative writing skills will be tested. Your ability to learn techniques from established writers will be important.

English Literature coursework

♦ If you are following **English Literature Specification A**, you will study and write about a prose text. This could be a pre-1914 or post-1914 text, balanced against the prose text that you will study for the examination.

♦ If you are following **English Literature Specification B**, you will study and write about a pre-1914 prose text. You will also complete a 'wider reading' written task, which will be based on prose, poetry or drama.

English Literature examination

♦ If you are following **English Literature Specification A**, you will study and write about a pre-1914 or post-1914 prose text (the opposite of your coursework category). You will be required to read closely and respond to a printed extract from your set text. You will also have to do an extended piece of writing on this set text.

♦ If you are following **English Literature Specification B**, you have to answer two questions on the prose section of your WJEC anthology. The first involves close reading of an extract from the anthology. The second offers a choice of tasks involving the comparison of some short stories from the anthology.

SUMMARY

♦ In English, the study of prose generally helps you develop reading and writing skills.

♦ In English Literature, you must show knowledge and understanding of whole texts.

Making the grade in prose coursework

G > F > E

Students need to have a sound general understanding of the text(s); be reasonably clear about what happens in them; and be able to pick out important details.

In English (response to prose), students are expected at grade 'E' to show familiarity when describing:

- ♣ the nature of the text's subject matter;
- ♣ the variety of character, situation, narration;
- ♣ the impact on the reader.

In English Literature (making comparisons), if comparing short stories, students are expected at grade 'E' to go beyond straightforward connections. They should begin to develop simpler points of comparison.

E > D > C

Students need to make sensible, detailed responses to the text(s), referring to the language, the structure, and the themes.

In English (response to prose), students are expected at grade 'C' to show insight when discussing:

- ♣ the nature of the text, its implications and relevance;
- ♣ style, structure and characters;
- ♣ the writer's characteristic use of language.

In English Literature (making comparisons), if comparing short stories, students are expected at grade 'C' to explore connections and comparisons, e.g. of theme and style.

C > B > A > A*

Students need to develop their ideas perceptively and confidently, with subtlety and precision. They must explore and interpret independently and with individuality.

In English (response to prose), students are expected at grade 'A*' to show originality of analysis and interpretation when evaluating:

- ♣ the moral, philosophical or social significance of the text;
- ♣ the writer's narrative craft and appeal to the reader;
- ♣ the patterns and details of words and images.

In English Literature (making comparisons), if comparing short stories, students are expected at grade 'A*' to probe and explore subtle points of comparison.

What's in a story?

Use the headings and questions below to stimulate interest in and understanding of the text that you are studying. Discuss and make notes. Do not settle for short answers – develop your thoughts.

The opening
How does the story start? What is the very first paragraph or page made up of? How are you drawn into the story? What holds your attention? How much does the writer tell you? Is it possible to tell how the story will develop?

The setting
Where does the story take place? Does the writer hint at the place or describe it in detail? Is it a familiar kind of setting or somewhere more imaginative? Is there a particular setting (or location) or are there several? What is the importance of the setting to the story as a whole? Is the setting just part of the background? Does the setting create a mood or atmosphere? What is the mood or atmosphere of the story?

The action
What happens in the story? What are the key events? How do they link together as a plot? Are there twists and cliffhangers? Is there a fast-moving plot or a steady build-up of suspense? What period of time is covered by the story – a few days or less? A year or more? Does the writer create a mystery by holding back information from the reader? Does the writer deliberately complicate the story or is it a fairly simple forward-moving sequence of events? Is the story easy or hard to believe in?

The characters
Who are the main characters in the story? Are there interesting minor characters who appear in the story? Is there one character who stands out above the rest as the main focus of our interest? How does the writer present the character(s) to us – through description, personality, dialogue, actions? What do you find interesting about the main character(s)? Are there interesting conflicts and relationships between characters? How do the characters develop and change, if at all, through the story?

The narrator
Who tells the story? Is it a first-person narrator (a character in the story) or a third-person narrator (an observer of the action from outside the story)? Is the narrator an important part of the particular story you are studying? Does the narrator have a distinct voice with any obvious features of language, such as dialect? Does the storyteller involve us closely in the story? Does the storyteller have a clear attitude to events and characters? Is the storyteller, in effect, a main character in the story?

The ending
How does the story end? Is it a satisfying ending that suits the type of story? Does the story end as you expect? Is it an open ending in any way? Does the writer leave questions unanswered about characters and themes? Does the writer pull all the loose ends together at the end to complete the story? Has the mood and atmosphere changed during the story?

The writer's skills

What do you appreciate and admire about the way the writer has written the story? Which writing skills or techniques stand out as memorable? Does the writer appear to have special skills in the description of people and places, dialogue, the presentation of feelings and attitudes (getting under the skin of characters), organizing a plot cleverly? Does the writer have wit? Does the writer create tension and atmosphere? Does the writer have a style of writing that has particular features? Is it noted for its rich range of language, description, and imagery? Is it particularly clear and direct?

The writer's ideas

What themes is the writer interested in? What is the writer perhaps trying to say about life, people, the world at large? If the writer belongs to the past, are the ideas still relevant? In what ways have attitudes changed (or are changing)? What is the writer trying to get you to understand? Is the writer optimistic (full of hope) or pessimistic (not hopeful) about the ideas he or she is expressing in the story?

The time in which it was written/is set

Is the story set in modern times or in the past? How distant from today does the story appear? If it is a pre-1914 story, what does it reveal about the time in which it was written? Are there any features of traditional storytelling – perhaps a more leisurely style? If it is a post-1914 story, does it represent a modern world? Are there any features of modern storytelling – perhaps a more direct, urgent style?

The reader

What is your considered personal response after reading the story? Have you learned anything from the text? Has it changed (or perhaps confirmed) your opinions in any way? What is your attitude to the writer after reading the story?

Armed with notes and opinions, you are now ready to organize an essay on the story or stories that you have studied. Consider your notes as very useful, but be prepared to drop those that have nothing to contribute to your response to an essay question. On the other hand, make sure that you keep going back to them as you write your essay, so that your best ideas are not left out.

Writing a coursework essay on prose

Here is a checklist of tips and warnings:

✓ Your essay needs a good sense of purpose from the start, so include an idea or opinion in the opening paragraph. Don't waste your first paragraph on a polite introduction. Respond to the task or question right from the start.

✓ Make sure your essay consists of reasonably well-developed paragraphs of fairly even length, typically about three to a page. Make sure your final paragraph – the conclusion – avoids exact repetition of points made previously.

✓ The coverage of a long text (a novel or short story) has to be highly selective. Don't resort to just telling the story. Selection is critical. If you are writing about a theme or a character, you need to choose the parts of the text that best support the points that you want to make. You need to be able to nip around the text picking out key features.

✓ You may also want to settle on one part of the text which you have decided has extra importance for your case. Is there a part of your essay that concentrates on one incident from the text and explores it?

✓ Your essay should contain detailed references to the text, including quotations. Quotations should be as short as possible - often a word, frequently a phrase, sometimes a sentence. Do not copy out a chunk of text to make your essay seem longer! Keep the flow of your essay going by quoting and commenting efficiently.

✓ Show that you are comfortable discussing the ideas and themes that the writer is presenting. Don't be afraid to have ideas. Write in standard English, but express yourself clearly, trying to explain what the whole text and its parts mean to you.

✓ If you have two short stories to write about, all of the above points about coverage, balance, and length still apply, but you also need a strategy for making comparative points. After your brief introduction, settle on one story and write about it thoughtfully for no more than a couple of pages. Then move on to your second story, treating it similarly but adding points of comparison and contrast where it is comfortable to do so. Round off your essay with a natural conclusion on both stories, with a main point of connection between the two.

✓ You need to aim for an essay of about 3-5 sides of file paper (average-sized handwriting). Anything much less than 3 sides is likely to be not detailed enough. Anything longer than 5 sides may be long-winded – the best candidates are sharp and selective with their ideas.

As you write your essay, judge its quality against this checklist.

Sample prose essay highlights (making comparisons)

Below are *extracts* from a very engaging essay by Pei Kei Sung, a GCSE student. Less than half of the essay is reproduced here. Read it and discuss its qualities – what 'A' grade potential does it have? Has it any weaknesses?

'Compare and contrast any two of the nineteenth-century mystery stories you have read.'

I was attracted to 'The Red Room' by H.G. Wells because of its unusual opening scene with three strange old people. The whole text is written in first-person narrative which allows the author to omit certain key details because only one person's viewpoint and feelings are conveyed.

The setting first appears to be a haunted house, but we later discover that it is a castle. The narrator is a man, presumably, who has decided to pay a visit to this castle and its supposedly haunted room, the red room. The narrator adopts a sceptical attitude to the existence of a ghost at the beginning, but after reading the story I believe that he said that 'it would take a very tangible ghost' to frighten him to reassure himself more than anything.

The man with the withered arm answers the narrator, reminding him that it is his choice to visit this red room and his choice only.... so if anything goes wrong only he himself is to be blamed. The narrator once again reassures himself that in all his years he has never seen a ghost and that he's unlikely to tonight. The old woman points out that he hasn't spent his years in the castle, but the narrator says that he can only become wiser if he confronts the ghost.

H.G. Wells manages to create a more eerie atmosphere by exaggerating things. This I have noticed is a key factor in this particular mystery story. The narrator detects a person coming down the corridor by the sound of a stick and a shambling step. The way this person walks suggests that he or she is nervous or unstable as if in a state of shock. The person enters the room and turns out to be a man living in the castle. The narrator describes this second old man, again nameless, the way his one eye is patched up, his teeth decaying and yellow and the fact that he relies on a single crutch. This produces a pirate-like figure although considerably more worn out. The reader begins to question what three so strange and remote creatures are doing together. What their former occupation was and more interestingly how the second old man came to be there? The narrator successfully leads us into his 'false trap' by making us question about the second man who turns out to be almost irrelevant to the story.

The narrator decides that he might as well visit this red room while he's there, so he takes a candle from the passage outside the room and proceeds down the passage. The flickering light of the candle would cast shadows of haunting figures on the cold, damp walls. I have also noticed that Wells deliberately places the red room far away from the cosy housekeeper's room so that if something does happen to him he is far from help and would probably be left there for some time. The narrator's walk through the corridors also helps to bide time and along with the various tricks played by the flickering light stimulates the reader to form his own thoughts and opinions on what is to happen next. I think this is effective in creating a sense of fear and apprehension...

...The second story, 'The Signalman' is also written in first-person narrative. Dickens begins with a cry of 'Halloa! Below there!' and then proceeds to launch into a description of the signalman's reaction. I was drawn into this story by the setting – a lonesome railway line – and the peculiar actions of the signalman.

Once again the author refrains from detailing us with the particulars of the narrator. However, unlike the previous story where we learned that the central character was visiting the castle's red room to satisfy himself about the circumstances surrounding his uncle's death, we don't actually learn any hard facts about the signalman's visitor, except that he too was once limited by his life, but now he is a free man – perhaps he is a doctor? His rational manner supports this theory...

...Both of these stories included a cautious yet curious narrator. Dickens and Wells were able to write in a style which really convinced the reader that they were a part of the story, experiencing the feelings of fear, curiosity and apprehension that were important to the overall effect of the stories.

Reading the stories from this book has made me realize how much mystery stories have changed, or perhaps our expectations of them have over the last century. They all seemed to be based on the daily lives of people in that period of time, incidents which would seem almost normal to us. I also found that the stories were very predictable. I believe this is so because many authors have since borrowed these ideas as a basis for their stories, but nevertheless I still enjoyed them and now consider a mystery to be something which perplexes the reader and cannot be decided upon. It often opens up a whole host of questions, rarely with answers, other than those provided by the reader.

Empathy work

What is an empathy task in English and English Literature?

In an empathy task you have to respond imaginatively to a text. You have to imagine you are one of the characters and/or try to write like the author of the original text.

For example, imagine you are Eppie in 'Silas Marner'. At the end of the story you think back over events, starting with the day when Silas Marner's money was discovered in the gravel pit. Write down your thoughts and feelings about that day and about the most significant events from then until the end of the story. Remember how Eppie would speak when you write your answer.

Empathy tasks can limit your achievement, if you ignore all of this advice.

Look at the assessment criteria for the higher grades and consider how you will show deeper understanding of the character, writer, and context in your writing.

Empathy tasks are not soft options. You are working to meet the same assessment criteria as in a literature essay.

Consider the overall balance of your coursework folder(s). Do not overload with empathy responses. Most of your coursework pieces should be essays.

Empathy work is valid for English (Reading) and English Literature coursework, if it shows understanding of the text and is assessed properly.

Key points about empathy work

You should concentrate on creating the right 'voice' in your writing, i.e. the voice of the character or the style of the writer.

You should concentrate on the action and details of the text. Your task should take you back into the text.

Your task should be reasonably realistic. For example, Lennie in Of Mice and Men is illiterate, so he would not write a diary!

Avoid newspaper reports. Transactional tasks, like newspaper reports based on To Kill a Mockingbird, deflect you into designing pages and do not give you much chance to get into the private thoughts of characters.

Avoid empathizing with minor characters. Not enough is known about them.

ASSESSMENT OF EMPATHY – GRADING (QUICK CHECK)

G/F/E: A simple commentary based on the surface of the text.
E/D/C: A secure grasp of the narrative and establishing a sense of character and attitude.
C/B/A/A*: A perceptive understanding of character and attitude, with a convincing tone and voice.

Sample empathy response to a prose text

Talking in Whispers is a novel by James Watson. It is set in Chile during the 1970s. The country is being ruled by a brutal military dictatorship. Here, Andres Larreta has a chance, fleeting meeting with an American photographer who has taken pictures of the brutality:

> 'But now…a chance in a million, an encounter lasting no longer than two minutes had changed everything. He was in possession of something the military would like to get their hands on – proof of their brutality. What's more, Andres was witness to what the Black Berets had done to a citizen of the United States of America.
>
> The Americans don't pour millions of dollars into Chile for us to beat up their newspapermen. Andres was at the street corner, poised for flight. All at once he had a purpose, a direction, a next step. He tapped the camera reverently. Somehow I must contact the Resistance. What's in this camera might be just as valuable as bullets.'

The novel ends with the leader, General Zuckerman, suffering the embarrassment of a peaceful protest by the people at a football match against England at the national stadium.

The brief extracts on PCM 7b are from the very beginning and the end of a long imaginative response to *Talking in Whispers*. The piece was written by Nathan Davies, a GCSE student. Read it and discuss its possible merits and limitations. Are the echoes of Watson's style, the density of detail, the political understanding and the sense of drama enough to earn a high grade?

The Trial of General Zuckerman

It had been a short year. Too short, thought Cesar Zuckerman, as he sat facing the polished mahogany wood which formed his miniature prison in the high court of justice in Santiago. A year which had changed so much, in such a short time. As his empire had fallen around him, his escape to Brazil formed and executed. The United Nations interference, the democratic Chile having its rebirth, and his own chase across South America until capture. And now to be tried by his own countrymen for crimes against them. 'The end is nigh' a phrase often heard, did it ever seem so apt as now.

The prosecuting lawyer, carefully chosen for his ability, stood to address the court. There had not been many lawyers left anyway. After the Junta took control, anybody who thought for themselves was considered a 'risk' to security, and was dealt with accordingly. Lawyers included. If one had escaped detection, now was the time for his revenge.

'Honourable members of the court, and member of the United Nations, I shall, with your permission, begin the prosecution of General Cesar Zuckerman.'

All nodded. The United Nations had played an important part in the liberation of Chile. When Zuckerman had fled after the revolution of his people, the U.N. had 'helped' first by taking control, and now by restoring democracy.

'My first witness. Jack Normanton.'

Some doors opened in a side wall and Normanton emerged, escorted by two guards. Not the dreaded black berets, but United Nations soldiers, the same as the soldiers that stood behind Zuckerman. Normanton stood in the witness box...

...'We had to become undercover agents, and by raising civilian morale instead of pulling triggers, we succeeded in staging a civilian revolution. Zuckerman escaped.' He said those words as though he was spitting poison. 'And our friends of the U.N. intervened. As they say, the rest is history.'

'Thank you' said the judge. For once he was doing the interrupting.

'We will break for lunch, and for our information to be absorbed.'

The Judge was the last to leave the courtroom. This trial would continue for weeks, more likely months. It would continue until every murder, every shooting, every disappearance had been brought to the court's view. Zuckerman truly would pay double for every tear shed. That song by Chico Barque was ludicrously true. Yet this judge wished one other witness could be called. Andres Larreta. So far he had sprung up everywhere. He was an integral part. He could hold vital evidence, but he was unknown, a missing link. He had his own story, but that would have to wait. Yes, it would have to wait...

Pre-1914 prose

FRANKENSTEIN BY MARY SHELLEY

Frankenstein, a young but brilliant scientist, creates a monster from the body parts of dead men. His monster, confused and angry, is brought to life and wreaks terrible havoc by murdering the people around him.

In the extract below, Frankenstein's monster is completed and it comes to life. Frankenstein is horrified by his creation and in terror he runs from it.

Chapter 5

It was on a dreary night of November that I beheld the accomplishment of my toils. With an anxiety that almost amounted to agony, I collected the instruments of life around me, that I might infuse a spark of being into the lifeless thing that lay at my feet. It was already one in the morning; the rain pattered dismally against the panes, and my candle was nearly burnt out, when, by the dull glimmer of the half-extinguished light, I saw the dull yellow eye of the creature open; it breathed hard, and a convulsive motion agitated its limbs.

How can I describe my emotions at this catastrophe, or how delineate the wretch whom with such infinite pains and care I had endeavoured to form? His limbs were in proportion, and I had selected his features as beautiful. Beautiful! Great God! His yellow skin scarcely covered the work of muscles and arteries beneath; his hair was of a lustrous black, and flowing; his teeth of a pearly whiteness; but these luxuriances only formed a more horrid contrast with his watery eyes, that seemed almost of the same colour as the dun-white sockets in which they were set, his shrivelled complexion and straight black lips.

The different accidents of life are not so changeable as the feelings of human nature. I had worked hard for nearly two years, for the sole purpose of infusing life into an inanimate body. For this I had deprived myself of rest and health. I had desired it with an ardour that far exceeded moderation; but now that I had finished, the beauty of the dream vanished, and breathless horror and disgust filled my heart. Unable to endure the aspect of the being I had created, I rushed out of the room and continued a long time traversing my bedchamber, unable to compose my mind to sleep. At length lassitude succeeded to the tumult I had before endured, and I threw myself on the bed in my clothes, endeavouring to seek a few moments of forgetfulness. But it was in vain; I slept, indeed, but I was disturbed by the wildest dreams. I thought I saw Elizabeth, in the bloom of health, walking in the streets of Ingolstadt. Delighted and surprised, I embraced her, but as I imprinted the first kiss on her lips, they became livid with the hue of death; her features appeared to change, and I thought that I held the corpse of my dead mother in my arms; a shroud enveloped her form, and I saw the grave-worms crawling in the folds of the flannel. I started from my sleep with horror; a cold dew covered my forehead, my teeth chattered, and every limb became convulsed; when, by the dim and yellow light of the moon, as it forced its way through the window shutters, I beheld the wretch — the miserable monster whom I had created. He held up the curtain of the bed; and his eyes, if eyes they may be called, were fixed on me. His jaws opened, and he muttered some inarticulate sounds, while a grin wrinkled his cheeks. He might have spoken, but I did not hear; one hand was stretched out, seemingly to detain me, but I escaped and ran downstairs. I took refuge in the courtyard belonging to the house which I inhabited, where I remained during the rest of the night, walking up and down in the greatest agitation, listening attentively, catching and fearing each sound as if it were to announce the approach of the daemoniacal corpse to which I had so miserably given life.

Oh! No mortal could support the horror of that countenance. A mummy again endued with animation could not be so hideous as that wretch. I had gazed on him while unfinished; he was ugly then, but when those muscles and joints were rendered capable of motion, it became a thing such as even Dante could not have conceived.

I passed the night wretchedly. Sometimes my pulse beat so quickly and hardly that I felt the palpitation of every artery; at others, I nearly sank to the ground through languor and extreme weakness. Mingled with this horror, I felt the bitterness of disappointment; dreams that had been my food and pleasant rest for so long a space were now become a hell to me; and the change was so rapid, the overthrow so complete!

Morning, dismal and wet, at length dawned and discovered to my sleepless and aching eyes the church of Ingolstadt, its white steeple and clock, which indicated the sixth hour. The porter opened the gates of the court, which had that night been my asylum, and I issued into the streets, pacing them with quick steps, as if I sought to avoid the wretch whom I feared every turning of the street would present to my view. I did not dare return to the apartment which I inhabited, but felt impelled to hurry on, although drenched by the rain which poured from a black and comfortless sky.

USING FRANKENSTEIN BY MARY SHELLEY

To understand this book, you must explore:

- ♦ the images of death used in the extract and elsewhere in the novel;
- ♦ the changing thoughts and feelings of Frankenstein;
- ♦ the changing thoughts and feelings of Frankenstein's monster;
- ♦ the differing views of science and religion.

Make notes on these questions to ensure you have a thorough overview of the novel:

1. What are Frankenstein's thoughts before his creation comes to life?
2. How do Frankenstein's thoughts and behaviour change after the monster comes to life?
3. What are the thoughts of the monster when he is first created and how do these develop?
4. What are the different presentations of 'monsters' in this novel?
5. What is Elizabeth's role in the story?
6. What is the role of the De Lacey family?
7. How is the theme of friendship conveyed in the novel?
8. How is the contrast between science and nature conveyed?
9. How does Shelley feel towards the monster?
10. What are the consequences of Frankenstein giving life to his creation?
11. How does Shelley mock the scientists of her time?
12. What warning does Shelley offer scientists of our time?
13. How does Shelley use black comedy in her story?
14. How does Shelley challenge traditional views of religion?
15. What is the meaning of: *delineate, lassitude, tumult*? Find out the meaning of any other words you do not recognize.

See PCM 3 for further advice on how to explore a prose text.

With guidance from your teacher, choose **one** of the following essay questions for your English and/or English Literature folder.

- ▬ Read the extract on PCM 8. How does Frankenstein react to his monster once it has awakened? How do his thoughts and feelings change towards his creation throughout the novel?
- ▬ How does Mary Shelley encourage us to feel sympathy for Frankenstein's monster in the novel?

See PCM 4 for advice on writing essays.

USING FRANKENSTEIN BY MARY SHELLEY

Pre-1914 prose

A TALE OF TWO CITIES BY CHARLES DICKENS

This book is set in both France and England at the time of the French Revolution. Lucie Manette is romantically involved with Charles Darnay, an aristocrat who objects to the way the French peasants are treated. Charles is acquitted of treason because of Lucie's father's testimony, but he is eventually tried a second time and found guilty. Meanwhile, Lucie also influences Sydney Carton, a drunk and an attorney, so much so that he performs an outstanding act of kindness.

In the extract below, Carton returns to his lawyer's chambers to do more work. Stryver, a respectable attorney, is there and notes that Carton is drunk. Despite this, Carton works diligently throughout the night.

BOOK II

Chapter Five – **The Jackal**

Sydney Carton, idlest and most unpromising of men, was Stryver's great ally. What the two drank together, between Hilary Term and Michaelmas, might have floated a king's ship. Stryver never had a case in hand, anywhere, but Carton was there, with his hands in his pockets, staring at the ceiling of the court; they went the same Circuit, and even there they prolonged their usual orgies late into the night, and Carton was rumoured to be seen at broad day, going home stealthily and unsteadily to his lodgings, like a dissipated cat. At last, it began to get about, among such as were interested in the matter, that although Sydney Carton would never be a lion, he was an amazingly good jackal, and that he rendered suit and service to Stryver in that humble capacity.

'Ten o'clock, sir,' said the man at the tavern, whom he had charged to wake him – 'ten o'clock, sir.'

'*What's* the matter?'

'Ten o'clock, sir.'

'What do you mean? Ten o'clock at night?'

'Yes, sir. Your honour told me to call you.'

'Oh! I remember. Very well, very well.'

After a few dull efforts to get to sleep again, which the man dextrously combated by stirring the fire continuously for five minutes, he got up, tossed his hat on, and walked out. He turned into the Temple, and, having revived himself by twice pacing the pavements of King's Bench-walk and Paper-buildings, turned into the Stryver chambers.

The Stryver clerk, who never assisted at these conferences, had gone home, and the Stryver principal opened the door. He had his slippers on, and a loose bed-gown, and his throat was bare for his greater ease. He had that rather wild, strained, seared marking about the eyes, which may be observed in all free livers of his class, from the portrait of Jeffries downward, and which can be traced, under various disguises of Art, through the portraits of every Drinking Age.

'You are a little late, Memory,' said Stryver.

'About the usual time; it may be a quarter of an hour later.'

They went into a dingy room lined with books and littered with papers, where there was a blazing fire. A kettle steamed upon the hob, and in the midst of the wreck of papers a table shone, with plenty of wine upon it, and brandy, and rum, and sugar, and lemons.

'You have had your bottle, I perceive, Sydney.'

'Two to-night, I think. I have been dining with the day's client; or seeing him dine — it's all one!'

'That was a rare point, Sydney, that you brought to bear upon the identification. How did you come by it? When did it strike you?'

'I thought he was rather a handsome fellow, and I thought I should have been much the same sort of fellow, if I had had any luck.'

Mr. Stryver laughed till he shook his precocious paunch. 'You and your luck, Sydney! Get to work, get to work.'

Sullenly enough, the jackal loosened his dress, went into an adjoining room, and came back with a large jug of cold water, a basin, and a towel or two. Steeping the towels in the water, and partially wringing them out, he folded them on his head in a manner hideous to behold, sat down at the table, and said, 'Now I am ready!'

'Not much boiling down to be done to-night, Memory,' said Mr. Stryver, gaily, as he looked among his papers.

'How much?'

'Only two sets of them.'

'Give me the worst first.'

'There they are, Sydney. Fire away!'

The lion then composed himself on his back on a sofa on one side of the drinking-table, while the jackal sat at his own paper-bestrewn table proper, on the other side of it, with the bottles and glasses ready to his hand. Both resorted to the drinking-table without stint, but each in a different way; the lion for the most part reclining with his hands in his waistband, looking at the fire, or occasionally flirting with some lighter document; the jackal, with knitted brows and intent face, so deep in his task, that his eyes did not even follow the hand he stretched out for his glass — which often groped about, for a minute or more, before it found the glass for his lips. Two or three times, the matter in hand became so knotty, that the jackal found it imperative on him to get up, and steep his towels anew. From these pilgrimages to the jug and basin, he returned with such eccentricities of damp headgear as no words can describe; which were made the more ludicrous by his anxious gravity.

At length the jackal had got together a compact repast for the lion, and proceeded to offer it to him. The lion took it with care and caution, made his selections from it, and his remarks upon it, and the jackal assisted both. When the repast was fully discussed, the lion put his hands in his waistband again, and lay down to mediate. The jackal then invigorated himself with a bum for his throttle, and a fresh application to his head, and applied himself to the collection of a second meal; this was administered to the lion in the same manner, and was not disposed of until the clocks struck three in the morning.

USING A TALE OF TWO CITIES BY CHARLES DICKENS

To understand this book, you must explore:

♦ the social and historical context of the French Revolution (the peasants revolting against the French aristocracy);

♦ the relationship between Lucie Manette and Charles Darnay, and Lucie's influence on Sydney Carton;

♦ The similarities and differences between the two locations of England and France.

Make notes on these questions to ensure you have a thorough overview of the novel:

1. How does Dickens convey the themes of oppression and class struggle?
2. What is the significance of Mr Lorry's dream about the man who was buried alive?
3. How does Dickens convey the theme of escape in different ways?
4. How does Dickens convey the stark contrast between the rich people and the poor people?
5. How does Dickens convey a sense of fate and impending doom? How do the characters react to this?
6. Why does Sydney Carton decide that he does not like Charles Darnay when he first meets him?
7. What impact does Lucie Manette's love for her father have on her relationships with other characters?
8. Why does Carton drink so much?
9. How is Monsieur the Marquis portrayed? What are his attitudes to the peasants of France?
10. What is Monsieur the Marquis' reaction to Darnay's behaviour and attitudes?

See PCM 3 for further advice on how to explore a prose text.

With guidance from your teacher, choose **one** of the following essay questions for your English and/or English Literature folder.

▬ Read the extract on PCM 10. How typical is this behaviour of Sydney Carton? What impact do the events of the novel have on him?
▬ What is Charles Darnay's attitude in the novel towards his family and background? How do these views influence his actions?

See PCM 4 for advice on writing essays.

Pre-1914 prose

THE HOUND OF THE BASKERVILLES BY ARTHUR CONAN DOYLE

The Baskerville family has been haunted for centuries by the curse of the Hound of the Baskervilles, an evil hellhound that terrorizes and murders members of the family. When the latest victim, Sir Charles Baskerville, is discovered dead, Sherlock Holmes is enlisted to solve the mystery and save the life of Sir Charles's last remaining heir, Sir Henry Baskerville.

In the extract below, Sir Charles Baskerville's physician, Dr Mortimer, visits Sherlock Holmes. He reveals the events that lead to the discovery of Sir Charles's body and the mysterious circumstances surrounding his death. The doctor claims that beside the body was a set of footprints belonging to a hound, the Hound of the Baskervilles.

CHAPTER TWO

Dr Mortimer refolded his paper and replaced it in his pocket. 'Those are the public facts, Mr Holmes, in connection with the death of Sir Charles Baskerville.'

'I must thank you,' said Sherlock Holmes, 'for calling my attention to the case which certainly presents some features of interest. I had observed some newspaper comment at the time, but I was exceedingly preoccupied by the little affair of the Vatican cameos, and in my anxiety to oblige the Pope I lost touch with several interesting English cases. This article, you say, contains all the public facts?'

'It does.'

'Then let me have the private ones.' He leaned back, put his finger-tips together, and assumed his most impassive and judicial expression.

'In doing so,' said Dr Mortimer, who had begun to show signs of some strong emotion, 'I am telling that which I have not confided to anyone. My motive for withholding it from the coroner's inquiry is that a man of science shrinks from placing himself in the public position of seeming to endorse a popular superstition. I had the further motive that Baskerville Hall, as the paper says, would certainly remain untenanted if anything were done to increase its already rather grim reputation. For both these reasons I thought that I was justified in telling rather less than I knew, since no practical good could result from it, but with you there is no reason why I should not be perfectly frank.

'The moor is very sparsely inhabited, and those who live near each other are thrown very much together. For this reason I saw a good deal of Sir Charles Baskerville. With the exception of Mr Frankland, of Lafter Hall, and Mr Stapleton, the naturalist, there are no other men of education within many miles. Sir Charles was a retiring man, but the chance of his illness brought us together, and a community of interests in science kept us so. He had brought back much scientific information from South Africa, and many a charming evening we have spent together discussing the comparative anatomy of the Bushman and the Hottentot.

'Within the last few months it became increasingly plain to me that Sir Charles's nervous system was strained to breaking point. He had taken this legend which I have read you exceedingly to heart — so much so that, although he would walk in his own grounds, nothing would induce him to go out upon the moor at night. Incredible as it may appear to you, Mr Holmes, he was honestly convinced that a dreadful fate overhung his family, and certainly the records which he was able to give of his ancestors were not encouraging. The idea of some ghastly presence constantly haunted him, and on more than one occasion he asked me whether I had on my medical journeys at night ever seen any strange creature or heard the baying of a hound. The latter question he put to me several times, and always with a voice which vibrated with excitement.

'I can well remember driving up to his house in the evening, some three weeks before the fatal event. He chanced to be at his hall door. I had descended from my gig and was standing in front of him, when I saw his eyes fix themselves over my shoulder, and stare past me with an expression of the most dreadful horror. I whisked round and had just time to catch a glimpse of something which I took to be a large black calf passing at the head of the drive. So excited and alarmed was he that I was compelled to go down to the spot where the animal had been and look around for it. It was gone, however, and the incident appeared to make the worst impression on his mind. I stayed with him all the evening, and it was on that occasion, to explain the emotion which he had shown, that he confided to my keeping that narrative which I read to you when first I came. I mention this small episode because it assumes some importance in view of the tragedy which followed, but I was convinced at the time that the matter was entirely trivial and that his excitement had no justification.

'It was at my advice that Sir Charles was about to go to London. His heart was, I knew, affected, and the constant anxiety in which he lived, however chimerical the cause of it might be, was evidently having a serious effect upon his health. I thought that a few months among the distractions of town would send him back a new man. Mr Stapleton, a mutual friend, who was much concerned at his state of health, was of the same opinion. At the last instant came this terrible catastrophe.

'On the night of Sir Charles's death Barrymore the butler, who made the discovery, sent Perkins the groom on horseback to me, and as I was sitting up late I was able to reach Baskerville Hall within an hour of the event. I checked and corroborated all the facts which were mentioned at the inquest. I followed the footsteps down the Yew Alley, I saw the spot at the moor-gate where he seemed to have waited, I remarked the change in the shape of the prints after that point, I noted that there were no other footsteps save those of Barrymore on the soft gravel, and finally I carefully examined the body, which had not been touched until my arrival. Sir Charles lay on his face, his arms out, his fingers dug into the ground, and his features convulsed with some strong emotion to such an extent that I could hardly have sworn to his identity. There was certainly no physical injury of any kind. But one false statement was made by Barrymore at the inquest. He said that there were no traces upon the ground round the body. He did not observe any. But I did – some little distance off, but fresh and clear.'

'Footprints?'

'Footprints.'

'A man's or a woman's?'

Dr Mortimer looked strangely at us for an instant, and his voice sank almost to a whisper as he answered:

'Mr Holmes, they were the footprints of a gigantic hound!'

USING THE HOUND OF THE BASKERVILLES BY ARTHUR CONAN DOYLE

To understand this book, you must explore:

- ♣ how Conan Doyle creates an air of suspense and mystery in his story;
- ♣ how Watson becomes involved in events;
- ♣ how Holmes eventually solves the mystery;
- ♣ the roles of fear and the supernatural.

Make notes on these questions to ensure you have a thorough overview of the novel:

1. How is Holmes introduced to us at the beginning of the novel? How typical is this portrayal of Holmes compared to the rest of the novel?
2. How does the portrayal of Dr and Miss Stapleton change during the novel?
3. What is the effect of having the story told through Watson's eyes?
4. What is the effect of Dr Mortimer's description of the events surrounding the death of Sir Charles Baskerville?
5. How does Conan Doyle describe the Hound and what is its effect on the people who see it?
6. How does the author encourage the reader to shift their suspicions to different characters?
7. What is the effect of including Dr Watson's case notes as part of the story?
8. What is the effect of setting the story on the moors?
9. How predictable is the solution to the mystery of the Hound of the Baskervilles?

See PCM 3 for further advice on how to explore a prose text.

With guidance from your teacher, choose **one** of the following essay questions for your English and/or English Literature folder:

- ▭ Read the extract on PCM 12. How does this exchange prepare the reader for the events that follow?
- ▭ How do Watson's thoughts and feelings change throughout the novel and how do these changes influence the reader?

See PCM 4 for advice on writing essays.

FEVER PITCH BY NICK HORNBY

This semi-autobiography tells the story of an uncomplicated man who has a deep passion for football. His passion develops from his childhood into adulthood and he manages to charm everyone through his love of the game. Then he meets Sarah and their relationship develops in tandem with the success of Arsenal, his favourite team.

In the extract below, Hornby describes when he fell deeply in love. He takes the girl to Highbury and she perceives the occasion in a very different way to him. He then goes on to discuss the many other differences he has found between boys and girls.

BOYS AND GIRLS

Arsenal v. Leicester City
2.4.77

Our relationship – the first serious, long-term, stay-the-night, meet-the-family, what-about-kids-one-day sort of thing for either of us – was in part all about discovering for the first time the mysteries of our counterparts in the opposite sex. I had had girlfriends before, of course; but she and I had similar backgrounds and similar pretensions, similar interests and attitudes. Our differences, which were enormous, arose mostly because of our genders; if I had been born a girl, she was the sort of girl, I realized and hoped, that I would have been. It was probably for this reason that I was so intrigued by her tastes and whims and fancies, and her belongings induced in me a fascination for girls' rooms that continued for as long as girls had rooms. (Now I am in my thirties they don't have rooms any more – they have flats or houses, and they are often shared with a man anyway. It is a sad loss.)

Her room helped me to understand that girls were much quirkier than boys, a realization that stung me. She had a collection of Yevtushenko's poems (who the hell was Yevtushenko?) and unfathomable obsessions with Anne Boleyn and the Brontes; she liked all the sensitive singer/songwriters, and was familiar with the ideas of Germaine Greer; she knew a little about paintings and classical music, knowledge gleaned from somewhere outside the A-level syllabus. How had that happened? How come I had to rely on a couple of Chandler paperbacks and the first Ramones album to provide me with some kind of identity? Girls' rooms provided countless clues to their character and background and tastes; boys, by contrast, were as interchangeable and unformed as foetuses, and their rooms, apart from the odd Athena poster here and there (I had a Rod Stewart poster on my wall, which I liked to think was aggressively, authentically and self-consciously down-market) were as blank as the womb.

It is true to say that most of us were defined only by the number and extent of our interests. Some boys had more records than others, and some knew more about football; some were interested in cars or rugby. We had passions instead of personalities, predictable and uninteresting passions at that, passions which could not reflect and illuminate us in the way that my girlfriend's did… and this is one of the most inexplicable differences between men and women.

I have met women who have loved football, and go to watch a number of games a season, but I have not yet met one who would make that Wednesday night trip to Plymouth. And I have met women who love music, and can tell their Mavis Staples from their Shirley Browns, but I have never met a woman with a huge and ever-expanding neurotically alphabetized record collection. They always seem to have lost their records, or to have relied on somebody else in the house – a boyfriend, a brother, a flatmate, usually a male – to have provided the physical details of their interests. Men cannot allow that to happen. (I am aware, sometimes, in my group of Arsenal-supporting friends, of an understated but noticeable jockeying: none of us likes to be told something about the club that we didn't know – an injury to one of the reserves, say, or an impending alteration to the shirt design, something crucial like that - by any of the others.) I am not saying that the anally retentive woman does not exist, but she is vastly outnumbered by her masculine equivalent; and while there are women with obsessions, they are usually, I think, obsessive about people, or the focus for the obsession changes frequently.

Remembering my late teens at college, when many of the boys were as colourless as tap water, it is tempting to believe that it all starts around that time, that men have had to develop their facility to store facts and records and football programmes to compensate for their lack of distinguishing wrinkles; but that doesn't explain how it is that one ordinary, bright teenager has already become more interesting than another ordinary, bright teenager, simply by virtue of her sex.

It is perhaps no wonder that my girlfriend wanted to come to Highbury: there wasn't really much else of me (she'd listened to my Ramones album), or at least nothing that I had yet discovered and extracted. I did have things that were mine – my friends, my relationships with my mum and my dad and my sister, my music, my love for cinema, my sense of humour – but I couldn't see that they amounted to very much that was individual, not in the way that her things were individual; but my solitary and intense devotion to Arsenal, and its attendant necessities (my vowel-mangling was by now at a point of almost intolerable crisis)… well, at least it had an edge to it, and gave me a couple of features other than a nose, two eyes and a mouth.

To understand this book, you must explore:
- ♣ Hornby's obsession with football;
- ♣ the use of wit and humour;
- ♣ the diary-type structure of the story.

Make notes on these questions to ensure you have a thorough overview of the novel:

1. What is Hornby's attitude towards his girlfriends in general?
2. How typical is Hornby of middle-class suburban males?
3. How does Hornby portray school life?
4. How typical a football fan is Hornby?
5. How important is the location of the story? Could it be written about any football team?
6. How does Hornby present his memories of football matches?
7. How does Hornby use humour to convey his messages?
8. How do Hornby's attitudes to relationships change?

See PCM 3 for further advice on how to explore a prose text.

With guidance from your teacher, choose **one** of the following essay questions for your English and/or English Literature folder:

▭ Read the extract on PCM 14. What are the differences that Hornby discovers between boys and girls and what impact do these have on the rest of the story?
▭ What do you learn about the male psyche from reading *Fever Pitch*?

See PCM 4 for advice on writing essays.

Post-1914 prose

ON THE BLACK HILL BY BRUCE CHATWIN

Identical twins Lewis and Benjamin Jones never leave their farmhouse on the border between Wales and England, and remain virtually untouched by the advances of the twentieth century. Their situation, having never moved from the place where they were born, invokes the sense of loneliness and tragedy of farm life, where their days are filled only with their farm work.

In the extract below, there is a serious fire. Their father Amos' consequent reaction to this causes their mother Mary to leave him, but only after he has physically assaulted her.

CHAPTER 16

Three years later, with a big bruise over her left eye, Mary wrote to her sister in Cheltenham stating her reasons for leaving Amos Jones.

She did not make excuses. Nor did she ask for sympathy. She simply asked shelter till she found herself a job. Yet, as she wrote, her tears made blotches on the notepaper, and she told herself that her marriage had not been doomed; that it could have worked; that they had both been in love and loved each other still; and that all of their troubles had begun with the fire.

Around eleven o'clock on the night of 2 October 1911, Amos had put away his carving chisels and was watching his wife sew the final stitches of a sampler, when Lewis ran downstairs shouting, 'Fire! There's a fire!'

Parting the curtains, they saw a red glow above the line of the cowshed roof. At the same moment, a column of sparks and flame shot upwards into the darkness.

'It's the ricks,' said Amos, and rushed outside.

He had two ricks on a patch of level ground between the buildings and the orchard.

The wind blew from the east and fanned the blaze. Wisps of burning hay flew up into the smokecloud, and fell. Frightened by the glare and the crackle, the animals panicked. The bull bellowed; horses stomped in their stalls; and the pigeons, pink in the flamelight, flew round and round in erratic circles.

Mary worked the pump-handle; and the twins carried the slopping pails to their father who was up a ladder, desperately trying to douse the thatch of the second rick. But the burning hay fell thicker and thicker, and that rick, too, was soon a crucible of flame.

The fire was seen for miles, and by the time Dai Morgan came up with his farm-servant, the sides of both ricks had caved in.

'Get out of my sight,' Amos snarled. He also shook off Mary as she tried to take his arm.

At dawn, a pall of grey smoke hung over the buildings, and Amos was nowhere to be seen. Stifled by the fumes, she called out fearfully, 'Amos? Amos? Answer me! Where are you?' – and found him, black in the face and beaten, slumped in the muck, against the pigsty wall.

'Do come inside,' she said. 'You must sleep now. There's nothing you can do.'

He gritted his teeth and said, 'I'll kill him.'

Obviously, he believed it was arson. Obviously, he believed that Watkins was the arsonist. But Mr Hudson, the constable, in charge of the case, was a bland, pink-faced fellow, who did not like interfering in a neighbours' quarrel. He suggested that the hay had been damp.

'Delayed combustion, most likely,' he said, doffing his cap and cocking his leg over his bicycle.

'I'll give him delayed combustion!' Amos reeled indoors, tramping mud over the kitchen floor. A teacup whizzed past Mary's head, smashed a pane of the china-cabinet and she knew that there were bad times on the way.

His hair fell out in handfuls. His cheeks became streaked with livid veins; and the blue eyes, once friendly, sank in their sockets and peered, as if down a tunnel, at a hostile world outside.

He never washed and seldom shaved – though that, in itself, was a relief; for when he whetted his razor, a look of such viciousness passed over his face that Mary held her breath and backed towards the door.

In bed, he used her roughly. To stifle her groans, he rammed his hand over her mouth. The boys, in their room along the landing, could hear her struggles and clung to one another.

He beat them for the smallest misdemeanour. He even beat them for speaking in a classy accent. They learned to rephrase their thoughts in the dialect of Radnorshire.

He only seemed to care, now, for his daughter – a wilful, mean-eyed child whose idea of fun was to pull the legs off daddy-long-legs. She had a head of flaming hair that licked downwards. He would dandle her on his knee and croon, 'You're the one as loves me. Ain't ye?' And Rebecca, who sensed Mary's lack of affection, would glare at her mother and brothers as if they were tribal enemies.

USING ON THE BLACK HILL BY BRUCE CHATWIN

To understand this book, you must explore:

- ♣ the different ideas of isolation;
- ♣ the connection between man and nature;
- ♣ the family life of the twins, both before and after their parents die.

Make notes on these questions to ensure you have a thorough overview of the novel:

1. How similar are the identical twins, Benjamin and Lewis?
2. How important is the location of the novel? What is the effect of this on the events and the characters?
3. How does Chatwin portray Wales in general?
4. What is the effect of the twins' isolation on their behaviour and relationships?
5. How is Amos Jones portrayed?
6. How is Mary Jones portrayed and how has she changed since her marriage to Amos?
7. What happens to the success and fortunes of the twins?
8. What happens to the success and fortunes of the Bickertons?
9. What opinions do the twins have of women?
10. How similar are the identical twins really? How do they differ?
11. What is the boys' relationship with their mother like?
12. Do you agree that the twins suffer from cultural isolation rather than social isolation? Explain your answer.
13. What is the effect of the names of the minor characters (e.g. Old Tom the coffin)?

See PCM 3 for further advice on how to explore a prose text.

With guidance from your teacher, choose **one** of the following essay questions for your English and/or English Literature folder.

- ▭ Read the extract on PCM 16. How typical is this behaviour of Amos Jones? What impact does his behaviour have on his two sons?
- ▭ How does the relationship between the people living in 'The Vision' and the people living in 'The Rock' change throughout the novel?

See PCM 4 for advice on writing essays.

Bad Blood by Lorna Sage

This is Sage's autobiography, charting her life from her earliest memories to her graduation from Durham University.

In the extract below, Sage describes her parents' marriage, particularly focusing on her impressions and memories of her father.

Chapter 8 – A Proper Marriage

Like many who'd married in the war, my parents were finding it hard to survive the peace. This wasn't because they had discovered that they didn't love each other once their life together wasn't spiced with constant separations and the threat of death. Far from it. But they had chosen each other so much against the social grain that they were tense, self-conscious, embattled, as though something was supposed to go wrong. Their families didn't like their marriage, nor did the village. Hanmer still lived in the era when most engagements were really contracts between legacies and land, abutting acres, second cousins twice removed, or at least a tied cottage and a tea service. The mythically egalitarian spirit of the Blitz only visited Hanmer in rumour, like the returning rumble of the odd bomber a bit off course on its way back from flattening Liverpool docks. A marriage between the vicar's daughter and the local haulier's son, who did his rounds in black face (A. Stockton & Sons hauled coal pre-war, mostly), was dangerous to decorum. You might think that if the haulier's boy went off to the wars a conscript private and came back a captain, this changed things. My parents' story could have been read as the triumphant progress of the sort of clean-cut local lad and younger son who does so well in folk tales. He falls in love with a dreamy virgin in thrall to her corrupt, spellbinding father; he goes away, wins his spurs in Normandy and the Ardennes, comes back to rescue her from the sterile, vicious vicarage and carries her off to realms of real life – the virtue, order and daylight decency of a proper marriage, and wholesome children. I think in some ways that's how they saw it themselves. However, Hanmer thought differently.

It was bad enough that my parents had gone out with each other in the 1930s, as teenagers. (This would have been a year or so after the Marj episode, Grandpa and Grandma were too busy rowing to care.) If they sat together into the small hours in the parked car he'd managed to borrow that was further scandalous evidence of my grandparents' indifference to propriety. No matter that these young people, Valma and Eric, deplored vicarage ways and were determinedly chaste; that – if gossip had credited it – would have been further evidence of their non-conformity. And the wrongness of it all was only compounded by my father's army career. The energy and ambition that took him to Sandhurst – where he learnt to his astonishment that the upper classes weren't cleverer after all – were suspect in Hanmer and so were warrior virtues, come to that, for this was largely a community of non-combatants and if you were unlucky enough to get conscripted, you kept your head down, joked with your mates and waited for it to be over.

This was what my father's elder brother Albert had done in North Africa. Almost the only leftover signs of Albert's sojourn in the desert were the beret he wore to deliver the coal and the belt he wore to hold up his trousers. Albert was an admirer of Winston Churchill, judging by the framed photo above the roll-top desk where he kept the sooty receipts, but he never talked about blood, toil, tears and sweat. Whereas for my father the war, the Royal Military College, his rise from the ranks, was an experience that remade him. He talked about his adventures on active service compulsively. He always maintained that he grew two extra inches, at eighteen, as a combined result of army PT and stopping carrying hundredweight sacks of coal for his father every day, as he'd done from the age of fourteen. It was a symbolic story. The army fathered him anew; he sprang full-grown out of the war. And he and my mother married in 1942, just before he got his commission.

He seemed an outsider after his years away, but in fact he was a native. His family lived in Horseman's Green, a hamlet just down the lane, where they owned a pretty square house, that had seen better days, called 'Ferncliffe', with a front garden, a farmyard where lorries left oily puddles and a couple of fields. He didn't seem much at home when we paid visits to his widowed mother (his father had died in 1943 not long after I was born) and Albert and their younger sister Binnie, and he probably hadn't been even before the war, when he'd had the assurance to start courting my mother.

When he was a boy, during the worst of the Depression, his parents had sent him to live with an aunt, while the other two stayed at home and this separation had left its mark. Later he'd been reclaimed, but not in spirit, although he laboured loyally for his father once he'd left school. A. Stockton & Sons had muddled along, carrying and delivering coal, sometimes cattle, sometimes labourers' worldly goods (giving the truck a hosing-down first) and doing a bit of farming or renting out a field on the side. At one stage they'd had a small shop too. When he and Albert came back from the army they inherited the remnants of this shapeless family firm and became partners. However, their attitudes to the enterprise were radically different. Uncle Albert, after the Sahara, was looking forward to muddling on as before. For my father muddle and compromise and inefficiency were the new enemy. A. Stockton & Sons became his peacetime 'company' and very soon he was giving the orders.

To understand this book, you must explore:
- Sage's family life – both with her grandparents and then with her parents;
- Sage's desire to be different, a misfit;
- Sage's almost Victorian style of up-bringing.

Make notes on these questions to ensure you have a thorough overview of the novel:

1. What are the impressions of Sage's parents? What impact did their absence in her early life have?
2. How important is the location of the novel?
3. How is the location described?
4. What impressions of relationships does Sage have during her formative years?
5. Who has the greatest influence on Sage's life?
6. How does Sage convey humour through the character of her mother?
7. What are Sage's views of her father?
8. How typical is Sage's teenage life?
9. How does Sage manage to surprise her family and the midwife after the birth of her baby?
10. What is the purpose of the Afterword?

See PCM 3 for further advice on how to explore a prose text.

With guidance from your teacher, choose **one** of the following essay questions for your English and/or English Literature folder:

- Read the extract on PCM 18. What memories does Sage have of her father? How does he differ from the other influential men in her life?
- What are Sage's memories of her grandparents in the book? How have they both shaped and influenced her life?

See PCM 4 for advice on writing essays.

Drama

Notes for teachers

Choice and range of drama
Speaking and Listening assessment
Planning considerations – organizing work on drama
       Reading and studying the texts in class
       Notes on using the photocopy masters (PCMs)
       The texts covered in this section

Photocopy masters (PCMs)

Notes for teachers
Choice and range of drama

All GCSE English candidates (for both the Wales and the England coursework options) have to study one play for coursework, while GCSE English Literature candidates for both Specification A and Specification B must study a pre-1914 and a post-1914 drama text (one for coursework and one for the examination). In most situations, teachers will want to integrate the English and the English Literature requirements to manage the workload for their students. (NB English Literature Specification B candidates may study a further play to fit the Wider Reading coursework category.)

English-only students at GCSE following the England coursework option must study a Shakespeare play, while those following the Wales coursework option choose to study a play, as part of a pair of drama and poetry Reading responses, with either a Welsh relevance or from different cultures and traditions.

Clearly, teachers entering students for both English and English Literature must plan carefully from the start of the course. Below are some possible combinations of drama texts for consideration:

	Coursework option for English	English coursework	English Literature coursework	English Literature examination
1.	ENGLAND	Shakespeare *(The Merchant of Venice, Romeo and Juliet, The Tempest)*	Post-1914 choice	Pre-1914 choice – Shakespeare *(The Merchant of Venice, Romeo and Juliet, The Tempest)*
2.	ENGLAND	Shakespeare	Pre-1914 choice (Shakespeare)	Post-1914 choice *(Hobson's Choice, A View From The Bridge, An Inspector Calls, Blood Brothers, Under Milk Wood)*
3.	WALES	Welsh relevance *(Under Milk Wood)*	Pre-1914 choice (Shakespeare)	Post-1914 choice *(Under Milk Wood)*
4.	WALES	Welsh relevance	Post-1914 choice (Welsh relevance)	Pre-1914 choice – Shakespeare *(The Merchant of Venice, Romeo and Juliet, The Tempest)*
5.	WALES	Different cultures and traditions *(A View From The Bridge)*	Pre-1914 choice (Shakespeare)	Post-1914 choice *(A View From The Bridge)*
6.	WALES	Different cultures and traditions	Post-1914 choice (Different cultures and traditions)	Pre-1914 choice - Shakespeare *(The Merchant of Venice, Romeo and Juliet, The Tempest)*

This is by no means an exhaustive list of combinations, but the above table recognizes that, in practice, most teachers will regard Shakespeare as their preferred choice for pre-1914 drama, and that few pre-1914 drama texts in the 'different cultures and traditions' and 'Welsh relevance' categories are viable options for most candidates.

In the above table, the shaded categories indicate choices of texts that can be made EITHER from this section OR from the teacher's own stock of ideas OR from the prescribed texts for English Literature (provided the coverage requirements are met).

In this section of the coursework guide, there are two texts in each of the following categories: pre-1914, post-1914, drama from different cultures and traditions, and drama with Welsh relevance. In keeping with the likely preferences of teachers, both of the pre-1914 texts are Shakespeare plays and all of the Welsh relevance and different cultures and traditions texts are post-1914 choices.

Speaking and Listening assessment

The study of drama texts is likely to contribute significantly to the Speaking and Listening element of the GCSE English course. The area of 'drama-focused activities' offers students the opportunity to work 'in a role presenting a character other than oneself', whether during improvization, hot-seating or taking part in a scripted scene. This could also include different interpretations or direction of a scene.

Notionally, one-third of Speaking and Listening assessment should be based on 'drama-focused activities'.

Planning considerations – organizing work on drama

Reading and studying the texts in class

The study of drama text(s) should be made as different as possible from the study of prose. For the potential high-achievers, the proper use of the language of drama and an implicit understanding of the theatre are realistic objectives; for the broad ability range (i.e. below the very best) a genuinely personal response is desirable and may be dependent on the words on the page being brought to life in performance. 'Story', 'plot', 'character' is language common to both drama and prose; 'audience', 'scene', 'act' is language that begins to create the sense of drama. At a simplistic level of engagement, students should be referring to 'audience' rather than 'reader', and 'play' rather than 'book'.

A class 'reading', moving towards 'performance', should contribute to students' experience of the play. The effort made to rearrange the furniture in the classroom and get the students on their feet will pay dividends – if the entrances, exits and asides are honoured by some attempt at staging, and some effort at positioning the 'actors', then students may get a 3D perspective of the action of the play and will start to think in terms of alternative readings. In a typical classroom setting, with students seated, the visual distinction between a Macbeth soliloquy and the public nature, of, say, the banquet scene will be lost. In a classroom 'performance', however modest the acting or reading, understanding of the plot will be tied into the comings and goings of the characters.

The video player (and the audiocassette player too) is an essential piece of equipment these days. Used often just as a means of covering the ground of the text – an alternative or a supplement to the class 'reading' – its potential for aiding the detailed study of extracts is now being exploited more frequently by teachers. Repeated plays of key speeches will push students towards some analysis of language; the same scene from different video productions will help emphasize the drama text as a blueprint for performance. Video used immediately before or after the classroom reading of extracts will keep students thinking about issues relating to impending coursework tasks.

Drama may include plays for film and television. However, work based on a viewing of taped or live performances must be linked to the study of the written text. Candidates will be expected to study a whole play, though the assignment may focus on specific aspects.

Notes on using the photocopy masters (PCMs)

PCMs 1-6 provide general information for students, which can be used at an individual teacher's discretion. PCM 1 explains the position of drama within the English and English Literature courses, and PCM 2 explains the grading structure and relevant assessment criteria for students, focussing on the English (response to drama) criteria. PCM 3 provides general guidance when reading and responding to any drama text, and will be a useful reference tool for students when they begin work on the task sheets. Similarly, PCM 4 will be a useful reference and checklist as students begin to draft out their own coursework essays. This checklist is followed by extracts from a sample student essay (PCM 5), which can be used as a practical discussion exercise about good and bad points before students begin their own work. PCM 6 provides a student example of an empathy task for evaluation and discussion.

The texts covered in this section

There are eight drama texts covered in this section (on PCMs 7-22). The task sheet for each text is preceded by a PCM with an extract from the text concerned. Each task sheet contains a number of supporting prompt questions to ensure that the student has a thorough knowledge of the text as a whole before beginning their essay task proper. Two main tasks then follow for students to choose from with guidance from their teacher. The first task option in each case makes use of the extract on the preceding PCM as a framework and then broadens out to deal with the text as a whole. The second task option is a self-standing examination of one aspect of the complete text. Teachers can, obviously, adapt these tasks if so desired, or add additional options of their own.

Where drama fits into your course

English coursework (Reading)

- In the ENGLAND coursework option, you have to study a Shakespeare play.
- In the WALES coursework option, you have to study either a play with Welsh relevance or one from different cultures and traditions (depending on the topic of your Reading assignment on poetry).

English coursework (Speaking and Listening)

- In Speaking and Listening, one of the three areas for assessment is **drama-focused activities**, for example, role play, hot-seating and/or scripted work.

English Literature coursework (Specifications A and B)

- You have to study either a pre-1914 play or a post-1914 play, depending on the text choice for the English Literature examination (see below).

English Literature examination (Specifications A and B)

- If you study a pre-1914 play for English Literature coursework, you must study a post-1914 play from the prescribed list of texts for the examination. If you study a post-1914 play for coursework, you must study a pre-1914 play for the examination.

English Literature coursework (Specification B only)

- You could choose to study another play for Wider Reading coursework.

SUMMARY

- You must study plays and write about them in both GCSE English and English Literature. You have to engage with drama-focused activities in Speaking and Listening (GCSE English).

Making the grade in drama coursework

G > F > E

Students need to have a sound general understanding of the play; be reasonably clear about what happens in it; and be able to pick out important details.

In English (response to drama), students are expected at grade 'E' to show familiarity when describing:
- the nature of the play, its meaning and ideas;
- the sequence of events and variety of characters;
- the impact on an audience.

E > D > C

Students need to make sensible, detailed responses to the text, referring to the language, the structure, and the themes.

In English (response to drama), students are expected at grade 'C' to show insight when discussing:
- the nature of the play, its implications, and relevance;
- characters, structure and stagecraft;
- use of language.

C > B > A > A*

Students need to develop their ideas perceptively and confidently, with subtlety and precision. They must explore and interpret independently and with individuality.

In English (response to drama), students are expected at grade 'A*' to show originality of analysis and interpretation when evaluating:
- the play's moral, philosophical or social significance
- stagecraft and appeal to an audience
- the patterns and details of words and images.

What's in a play?

Use the headings and questions below to stimulate interest in and understanding of the play that you are studying. Discuss and make notes. Do not settle for short answers – develop your thoughts.

The opening scene(s)
How does the play start? What is in the very first scene? Is it a low-key or a highly dramatic opening? How are you drawn into the action? What holds your attention? How much does the writer tell you? Is it possible to tell how the plot will develop?

The setting
Where does the action take place? Does the writer describe it in detail? Is the stage expected to be very precisely arranged? What is the importance of the setting to the story as a whole? Is the setting just part of the background? Does the setting create a mood or atmosphere? What is the mood or atmosphere of the play? What theatrical tricks or surprises are evident?

The action
What happens in the play? What are the key events? How do they link together as a plot? Are there twists and cliffhangers? Is there a fast-moving plot or a steady build-up of suspense? What period of time is covered by the action – a few days or less? A year or more? Does the writer create a mystery by holding back information from the reader? Which action takes place with the audience understanding everything and the character(s) ignorant of the truth (dramatic irony)? Does the writer deliberately complicate the action or is it a fairly simple forward-moving sequence of events? Is the action easy or hard to believe in?

The characters
Who are the main characters in the play? Are there interesting minor characters who appear in the play? Is there one character who stands out above the rest as the main focus of our interest? How does the writer present the character(s) to us – through description, personality, dialogue, actions? What do you find interesting about the main character(s)? Are there interesting conflicts and relationships between characters? How do the characters develop and change, if at all, through the play?

The structure of the play
How many acts and scenes are there in the play? Is there a prologue and/or epilogue? Is the play heavy or light on stage directions? Is there a narrator (or a character with the role of narrator)? Is there a main character who speaks innermost thoughts at length in a soliloquy? Is there a clear conflict of ideas running through the play? Is there more than one plot (a main plot with sub-plots)? Are there key moments of dramatic irony, when the audience understands, but not the character(s)? How does the play build up to its climax? How is the conflict resolved?

The ending

How does the play end? Is it a satisfying ending that suits the type of play? Does the play end as you expect? Is it an open ending in any way? Does the writer leave questions unanswered about characters and themes? Does the writer pull all the loose ends together at the end to complete the play? Has the mood and atmosphere changed during the play?

The writer's skills

What do you appreciate and admire about the way the writer has created the play? Which dramatic skills or techniques stand out as memorable? Does the writer appear to have special skills in visual drama, characterization, scenes of conflict, the presentation of feelings and attitudes (getting under the skin of characters), creating memorable minor characters, organizing a plot cleverly, using theatrical effects? Does the writer have wit? Does the writer create suspense?

The writer's ideas

What themes is the writer interested in? What is the writer perhaps trying to say about life, people, the world at large? If the writer belongs to the past, are the ideas still relevant? In what ways have attitudes changed (or are changing)? What is the writer trying to get you to understand? Is the writer optimistic (full of hope) or pessimistic (not hopeful) about the ideas he or she is expressing in the play?

The time in which it was written/is set

Is the play set in modern times or in the past? How distant from today does the play appear? If it is a Shakespeare play, what does it reveal about the attitudes of his age? In what ways are Shakespeare's characters timeless, showing unchanging human characteristics? If it is a post-1914 play, does it represent a modern world? Is there a particularly modern conflict or dilemma at the heart of the play? Do the characters behave in a way that people of bygone ages would fail to understand?

The reader

What is your considered personal response after watching and studying the play? Have you learned anything from the play? Has it changed (or perhaps confirmed) your opinions in any way? How did you feel watching it and, now, having studied it? What is your attitude to the writer after studying the play?

Armed with notes and opinions, you are now ready to organize an essay on the play that you have studied. Consider your notes as very useful, but be prepared to drop those that have nothing to contribute to your response to an essay question. On the other hand, make sure that you keep going back to them as you write your essay, so that your best ideas are not left out.

Writing a coursework essay on drama

Here is a checklist of tips and warnings:

✔ When you write about drama, remember to refer to the **play** (not the book or novel), the **audience** (not the reader), and the **scene** or **act** (not the chapter).

✔ Use the straightforward language of drama: **dialogue**, **action**, **voice**, **movement**, **tension**, **stage directions**. Try to keep in mind a sense of the play **as a drama**, more than a story.

✔ Your essay needs a good sense of purpose from the start, so include an idea or opinion in the opening paragraph. Don't waste your first paragraph on a polite introduction. Respond to the task or question right from the start.

✔ Make sure your essay consists of reasonably well-developed paragraphs of fairly even length, typically about three to a page. Make sure your final paragraph – the conclusion – avoids exact repetition of points made previously.

✔ The coverage of a long play has to be highly selective. Don't resort to just telling the story. Selection is critical. If you are writing about a theme or a character, you need to choose the parts of the play that best support the points that you want to make. You need to be able to nip around the play picking out key features.

✔ You may also want to settle on one scene that you have decided has extra importance for your case. Is there a part of your essay that perhaps concentrates on one particular scene and explores it?

✔ Your essay should contain detailed references to the play, including quotations. Quotations should be as short as possible – often a word, frequently a phrase, sometimes a sentence. Do not copy out a chunk of text to make your essay seem longer! Keep the flow of your essay going by quoting and commenting efficiently.

✔ Show that you are comfortable discussing the ideas and themes that the writer is presenting. Don't be afraid to have ideas. Write in standard English, but express yourself clearly, trying to explain what the whole play and its parts mean to you.

✔ You need to aim for an essay of about 3-5 sides of file paper (average-sized handwriting). Anything much less than 3 sides is likely to be not detailed enough. Anything longer than 5 sides may be long-winded – the best candidates are sharp and selective with their ideas.

As you write your essay, judge its quality against this checklist.

Sample drama essay highlights

The **extracts** below are from an essay by Steven Sanders, a GCSE student, on *As You Like It*, a Shakespearean comedy. In this essay he grapples with the fact that the play can be genuinely funny, yet in production it also has its dark, ominous side.

'How interesting and amusing is *As You Like It* today?'

(This extract deals with the visual impact; the sense of comedy; the understanding of contrasts; the sense of theatre and lack of realism; the challenge to the audience.)

...As You Like It relies heavily on human relationships and love, but it also shows us, the audience, the difference between life at the court and life in the forest or rural surrounds, a type of good versus evil, with the court being the bad side of the coin. This was shown in its extreme during the production I saw where life at court was depicted as something from the Mafia with Duke Frederick and his courtiers wearing dark suits, sunglasses and armed with a hand pistol each. This may appear to be slightly over the top, but I along with the majority of the audience found this entertaining and amusing. The producers wished to bring the play up-to-date without detracting from the text.

(There is some focus in this extract on a set-piece scene; good versus evil; the romantic theme; illusion and reality; staging; the visual impact; the action on stage; the sense of comedy.)

...One of the early scenes with potential for comedy and action on stage is the wrestling match between Charles and Orlando. This is not just exciting for the audience because it is man fighting against man, David versus Goliath once again, but also because of the build up prior to the fight, where Rosalind and Orlando first meet, and their pledges to each other immediately after the match. One can sense the feeling of love at first sight. This feeling is based upon the way the scene is acted and more importantly the dialogue between Rosalind and Orlando in which Rosalind speaks, passionately, the words 'The little strength that I have, I would it were with you'. At Stratford, the scene was played with a great deal of chemistry between Rosalind and Orlando and with a great deal of wit too. Charles the wrestler was played by an actor in a leopard skin and to look at him was funny in itself. The actual wrestling match took place on stage with spectators milling about and forming a human ring to surround the wrestlers. Of course, Orlando wins, which is far-fetched, but in line with the romantic atmosphere of the play...

(There is some focus here on a particular scene; on characters in opposition; a surprise element; wit in the dialogue; the pastoral/courtly theme.)

...The best example of this wit I feel occurs in Act 3 Scene 2 where Corin, a simple shepherd, and Touchstone, the court jester, enter in conversation. This scene may first appear very static, lacking movement and energy but when performed on stage the reverse is true. In this scene Touchstone criticizes Corin and attempts to gain a laugh for what he sees as a very narrow existence, proving his dislike for the country life. However, Corin is unnerved by Touchstone's remarks and fruitless comments as in the case of Stratford he (Corin) was the first to laugh with and at Touchstone. He also encouraged the audience to join in the laughter there. This is quite a reversal in fortunes for both characters in such a short space of time, rather unwittingly in Corin's case. Touchstone who would normally make people laugh is at the centre of the joke himself... Corin says, 'Those that are good manners at the court are as ridiculous in the country as the behaviour of the country is mockable at the court', going on to point out that kissing hands is not a particularly hygienic thing for shepherds to do!

(This extract deals with the strategic role of a particular character; sub-plots and unity.)

...Touchstone also plays an important role in the structure of the play. While other characters, or groups of characters, are playing their own parts, separated from each other, independently playing unrelated roles, Touchstone is familiar to all the cast and he gives the play a good feeling of integration. Without him the play would lose its feeling of unity and would break down into separate groups of characters...

These extracts show to an extent how difficult it is to write an essay both on the theatrical aspects of the play and the language of the play. Steven makes a concerted effort to focus on the question and to combine his experience of watching a performance and studying the text in class. It should be stressed that the task was a difficult one and that the job of the paragraphs above is to show a range of possibilities, rather than the perfect end-product. For instance, a task on Touchstone would be a more than sufficient challenge for most students, but the better answers would need to develop an understanding of his role as fool, his strategic role in the play and his wit (in some detail), as well as his fate as a character.

Sample empathy response to a play

UNDER MILK WOOD: EPITAPH

Kenneth Boyns, a GCSE student, wrote an imaginative response to *Under Milk Wood*, the famous radio play by Dylan Thomas. These opening extracts imitate the writer's (or the dual narrators') style successfully and supply rich echoes of textual detail. The piece, even in its shortened form, aspires to a high grade. How convincingly does it match the assessment criteria for English (response to drama)?

1st Voice   To begin not quite at the beginning, maybe eight long months, months of cold, rain, warmth, sun, falling leaves and failing winter sun from the beginning. In some small town, the same starless, moonless sky, with heavy snow clouds blotting out the heavens. Once again we penetrate the mind of this small town, the same blind houses stare not seeing out at the same fishing boat bobbing sea. The town sleeps once again, but this time one sleeps deeper than the rest, an inevitable sleep, a peaceful, dreamless sleep not disturbed by any human noise or worry.

The squat chapel somehow seems colder than before, and not because of time, the faint remnants of hymns and sermons long ago spoken, seem to float through the cold, cold air in this 'the one place of worship'. The 'neglected graveyard' somehow seems less neglected and dare it be said, waiting to welcome to the cold damp depths any mistaken soul and any human fool enough to die in this forsaken place.

Listen, once again time passes and the sky to the east lightens and the sun prepares for its daily performance of trying to break through and defeat its deadly enemy, to fight the brave and good fight to brighten up the day.

Listen, once again Captain Cat dreams, but another joins the list of acquaintances he has on the other side of the vast gulf. This night, as all others the drowned meet him in the dark depths and enter his mind.

2nd Voice   And Mr Pugh sighing and nodding his head remorselessly mumbles. And then he returns to the great depths and concocts deadly new brews in the hissing cauldron of death that his mind has become and he softly pads out of the room like a dog with its tail between its legs.

1st Voice   There is a strange silence over the town today, no organ being played by the dutiful Organ Morgan, no clattering milk bottles, collected by a dull and drab Olley Milkman, no nagging wives chattering in the square, no cheerful chatter by a nosey Willy

Willy, no sign of life...

Listen, the sound of feet and a sober Cherry Owen in a black suit enters through the door of the Sailor's Arms. As he does, lace curtains part as Willy Willy and other curious and wondering people look at the curious sight of Cherry Owen in a suit. For the first time in his life he enters into the Sailor's Arms not to get drunk, but to deliberately stay sober and as he enters he sighs a deep sigh and ducks under the low doorway.

2nd Voice Listen, the town is awakening, many come out from behind closed doors, but wait, all wear dark dull mourning colours, yes, mourning colours, mourning for the loss of one of their flock.

1st Voice The door of Bethesda House opens and the Reverend Eli Jenkins stands there in the open doorway in his preacher's black and flowing white hair looking the very picture of a long dead druid. He holds in one hand a large leather bound book and after looking around him he enters into the street.

2nd Voice As the good reverend enters into the street, the door of the Sailor's Arms opens and Sinbad Sailors and Cherry Owen come out of the Sailors Arms at the front of a coffin with two other good townsmen dressed in black carrying the morbid reminder of death and darkness. Inside the coffin, Mary Ann Sailors sleeps her last sleep and has left her dear paradise of Llareggub for the paradise of another place, an eternal paradise.

1st Voice The Reverend Eli Jenkins places himself at the head of the solemn and sober procession with the body of the heavenly ascended behind him. Behind the coffin proceed the dour faced people of the town, Captain Cat, Mr Mog Edwards, Mr Waldo again surprisingly sober, Mr Waldo's wife, Mrs Ogmore on her right and Mr Pritchard on her left. A respectful distance behind the tall figure of the haberdasher walks the dressmaker and sweet shopkeeper, Miss Myronwy Price. Her dreaming desire, Mr Mog Edwards, his rubber stamp and all, helps blind Captain Cat along, gently steering him into the chapel 'of no architectural interest', past the many tombstones, and through the large oak-door cut down from milk-wood, that once was blessed by the ancient druids and never again since...

Pre-1914 drama

HENRY V BY WILLIAM SHAKESPEARE

Henry V, the much-loved King of England, wants to claim the throne of France but his initial attempts fail and he is forced to fight the French to secure their crown. The Dauphin taunts Henry, but this merely serves to make Henry more determined to go into battle. A fierce war ensues and it is only when Henry is offered the hand of Princess Katharine of France that order is restored, with their son being made the heir to both the English and French crowns.

In the extract below, members of the French army are discussing the forthcoming battle. They delight in poking fun at the English and in particular at King Henry.

Act 3, Scene 8

Orléans	The Duke of Bourbon longs for morning.
Rambures	He longs to eat the English.
Constable	I think he will eat all he kills.
Orléans	By the white hand of my lady, he's a gallant prince.
Constable	Swear by her foot, that she may tread out the oath.
Orléans	He is simply the most active gentleman of France.
Constable	Doing is activity, and he will still be doing.
Orléans	He never did harm that I heard of.
Constable	Nor will do none tomorrow. He will keep that good name still.
Orléans	I know him to be valiant.
Constable	I was told that, by one that knows him better than you.
Orléans	What's he?
Constable	Marry, he told me so himself, and he said he cared not who knew it.
Orléans	He needs not, it is no hidden virtue in him.
Constable	By my faith, sir, but it is. Never anybody saw it but his lackey. 'Tis a hooded valour, and when it appears it will bate.
Orléans	Ill will never be said well.
Constable	I will cap that proverb with 'There is flattery in friendship'.
Orléans	And I will take up that with 'Give the devil his due'.
Constable	Well placed. There stands your friend for the devil. Have at the very eye of that proverb with 'A pox of the devil'.
Orléans	You are the better at proverbs, by how much 'a fool's bolt is soon shot'.
Constable	You have shot over.
Orléans	'Tis not the first time you were overshot.

Enter a Messenger.

Messenger	My lord High Constable, the English lie within fifteen hundred paces of your tents.
Constable	Who hath measured the ground?
Messenger	The lord Grandpré.
Constable	A valiant and most expert gentleman. Would it were day! Alas, poor Harry of England! He longs not for the dawning as we do.
Orléans	What a wretched and peevish fellow is this king of England, to mope with his fat-brained followers so far out of his knowledge.
Constable	If the English had any apprehension they would run away.
Orléans	That they lack, for if their heads had any intellectual armour they could never wear such heavy headpieces.
Rambures	That island of England breeds very valiant creatures. Their mastiffs are of unmatchable courage.
Orléans	Foolish curs, that run winking into the mouth of a Russian bear and have their heads crushed like rotten apples. You may as well say that's a valiant flea that dare eat his breakfast on the lip of a lion.
Constable	Just, just. And the men do sympathize with the mastiffs in robustious and rough coming on, leaving their wits with their wives. And then, give them great meals of beef and iron and steel, they will eat like wolves and fight like devils.
Orléans	Ay, but these English are shrewdly out of beef.
Constable	Then shall we find tomorrow they have only stomachs to eat and none to fight. Now is it time to arm. Come, shall we about it?
Orléans	It is now two o'clock. But let me see. By ten we shall have each a hundred Englishmen!

Exeunt

USING HENRY V BY WILLIAM SHAKESPEARE

To understand this play, you must explore:

♠ the idea of order and disorder as exemplified by the English and French respectively;
♠ the theme of reformation;
♠ the atmosphere of hostility produced by the conflict between England and France.

Make notes on these questions to ensure you have a thorough overview of the play:

1. What is the impact of the repeated references to '*wings*'?
2. What is the impact of the repeated references to wild animals?
3. What is the impact of the repeated references to the weather and natural disasters, e.g. earthquakes?
4. What is the impact on the audience of the long descriptions of the deaths of York and Suffolk?
5. Why does Henry disguise himself as a commoner and talk with the troops before the battle?
6. What is the impact of Henry's speech about the responsibilities of being a king?
7. How is Katharine portrayed in the play?
8. What is the purpose of the exchange between Katharine and Alice?
9. What is the role of Williams? What is the dramatic impact of the behaviour of this character?
10. What is the role of Fluellen? How is he portrayed?
11. What is the role of Pistol? How is he portrayed?
12. Why are Nym and Bardolph hanged?
13. What are the consequences of war, according to Shakespeare?

See PCM 3 for further advice on how to explore a play.

With guidance from your teacher, choose **one** of the following essay questions for your English and/or English Literature folder:

▭ Read the extract on PCM 7. What is the attitude of the French camp towards the approaching battle? How sensible is it to have this attitude towards the English army?
▭ How does Shakespeare use this play to demonstrate his patriotism for England?

See PCM 4 for advice on writing essays.

Pre-1914 drama

MUCH ADO ABOUT NOTHING BY WILLIAM SHAKESPEARE

This is an exploration of different attitudes to love and relationships. Claudio falls in love with the governor's daughter, Hero. However, the prince's evil brother conspires to convince Claudio that his beloved Hero has been unfaithful to him. It is up to the reluctant lovers, Benedick and Beatrice, to prove Hero's innocence.

In the extract below, Benedick and Beatrice are reunited after a battle. However, they are not pleased to see each other and immediately resort to exchanging witty insults in front of the entire party.

Act I Scene I

Benedick	If Signor Leonato be her father, she would not have his head on her shoulders for all Messina, as like him as she is.
Beatrice	I wonder that you will still be talking, Signor Benedick; nobody marks you.
Benedick	What, my dear Lady Disdain! Are you yet living?
Beatrice	Is it possible disdain should die while she hath such meat food to feed it as Signor Benedick? Courtesy itself must convert to disdain if you come in her presence.
Benedick	Then is courtesy a turncoat. But it is certain I am loved of all ladies, only you excepted. And I would I could find in my heart that I had not a hard heart, for truly I love none.
Beatrice	A dear happiness to women. They would else have been troubled with a pernicious suitor. I thank God and my cold blood I am of your humour for that. I had rather hear my dog bark at a crow than a man swear he loves me.
Benedick	God keep your ladyship still in that mind. So some gentleman or other shall scape a predestinate scratched face.
Beatrice	Scratching could not make it worse an 'twere such a face as yours were.
Benedick	Well, you are a rare parrot-teacher.
Beatrice	A bird of my tongue is better than a beast of yours.
Benedick	I would my horse had the speed of your tongue, and so good a continuer. But keep your way, o' God's name. I have done.
Beatrice	You always end with a jade's trick. I know you of old.
Don Pedro	This is the sum of all, Leonato. —Signor Claudio and Signor Benedick, my dear friend Leonato hath invited you all. I tell him we shall stay here at the least a month, and he heartily prays some occasion may detain us longer. I dare swear he is no hypocrite, but prays from his heart.

Leonato	If you swear, my lord, you shall not be forsworn. *(To Don John)* Let me bid you welcome, my lord. Being reconciled to the prince your brother, I owe you all duty.
Don John	I thank you. I am not of many words, but I thank you.
Leonato	*(To Don Pedro)* Please it your grace lead on?
Don Pedro	Your hand, Leonato. We will go together.

Exeunt all but Benedick and Claudio

Claudio	Benedick, didst thou note the daughter of Signor Leonato?
Benedick	I noted her not, but I looked on her.
Claudio	Is she not a modest young lady?
Benedick	Do you question me as an honest man should do, for my simple true judgement, or would you have me speak after my custom, as being a professed tyrant to their sex?
Claudio	No, I pray thee speak in sober judgement.
Benedick	Why, i' faith, methinks she's too low for a high praise, too brown for a fair praise, and too little for a great praise. Only this commendation I can afford her, that were she other than she is she were unhandsome, and being no other but as she is, I do not like her.
Claudio	Thou thinkest I am in sport. I pray thee tell me truly how thou likest her.
Benedick	Would you buy her, that you enquire after her?
Claudio	Can the world buy such a jewel?
Benedick	Yea, and a case to put it into. But speak you this with a sad brow, or do you play the flouting Jack, to tell us Cupid is a good hare-finder and Vulcan a rare carpenter? Come, in what key shall a man take you to go in the song?
Claudio	In mine eye she is the sweetest lady that ever I looked on.
Benedick	I can see yet without spectacles, and I see no such matter. There's her cousin, an she were not possessed with a fury, exceeds her as much in beauty as the first of May doth the last of December. But I hope you have no intent to turn husband, have you?
Claudio	I would scarce trust myself, though I had sworn the contrary, if Hero would be my wife.
Benedick	Is't come to this? In faith, hath not the world one man but he will wear his cap with suspicion? Shall I never see a bachelor of three-score again? Go to, i' faith, an thou wilt needs thrust thy neck into a yoke, wear the print of it, and sigh away Sundays.

USING MUCH ADO ABOUT NOTHING BY WILLIAM SHAKESPEARE

To understand this play, you must explore:

- ♠ the role of disguises and mistaken identity;
- ♠ the different attitudes to relationships;
- ♠ the battle of the sexes.

Make notes on these questions to ensure you have a thorough overview of the play:

1. How does Shakespeare explore the theme of love?
2. How does Shakespeare explore the idea of family loyalty?
3. What is the role of the masked ball?
4. How are Benedick and Beatrice tricked into falling in love?
5. What is Beatrice's relationship like with her cousin Hero?
6. How similar are Benedick and Beatrice?
7. How does Shakespeare add humour to the play?
8. What is the impact of the accusations against Hero? How does the audience feel?
9. What are the roles of Dogberry and Verges?
10. How does Margaret behave in the play? What is the audience's attitude towards her?
11. What is Don John's motive for his behaviour?
12. How does Claudio prove he is an honourable gentleman to Leonato?

See PCM 3 for further advice on how to explore a play.

With guidance from your teacher, choose **one** of the following essay questions for your English and/or English Literature folder:

▬ Read the extract on PCM 9. How typical is this behaviour of Benedick? How does he add humour to the play?

▬ How does Shakespeare explore the theme of faithfulness in *Much Ado About Nothing*?

See PCM 4 for advice on writing essays.

Post-1914 drama

EDUCATING RITA BY WILLY RUSSELL

Rita, a 26-year-old hairdresser, attends a literature course run by the Open University in an attempt to improve herself. Her teacher, Frank, is unconventional to say the least. Rita's initially fresh, original approach to her course becomes more constrained as she prepares for her exams.

In the extract below, Rita is late for her lesson with Frank because she has been talking to some other students. Her talk with them escalated into a full debate after she disagreed with one of the students' point of view. At the start of her lesson she recounts this event to Frank.

Act 2, Scene 2

The lights come up on Frank who is sitting at his desk marking an essay. Occasionally he makes a tutting sound and scribbles something. There is a knock at the door.

Frank   Come in.

Rita enters, closes the door, goes to the desk and dumps her bag on it. She takes her chair and places it next to Frank and sits down.

Rita   *(Talking in a peculiar voice)* Hello, Frank.

Frank   *(Without looking up)* Hello. Rita, you're late.

Rita   I know, Frank. I'm terribly sorry. It was unavoidable.

Frank   *(Looking up)* Was it really? What's wrong with your voice?

Rita   Nothing is wrong with it, Frank. I have merely decided to talk properly. As Trish says there is not a lot of point in discussing beautiful literature in an ugly voice.

Frank   You haven't got an ugly voice; at least you didn't have. Talk properly.

Rita   I am talking properly. I have to practise constantly, in everyday situations.

Frank   You mean you're going to talk like that for the rest of this tutorial?

Rita   Trish says that no matter how difficult I may find it I must persevere.

Frank   Well will you kindly tell Trish that I am not giving a tutorial to a Dalek?

Rita   I am not a Dalek.

Frank   *(Appealingly)* Rita, stop it!

Rita   But Frank, I have to persevere in order that I shall overcome.

Frank   Rita! Just be yourself.

Rita   *(Reverting to her normal voice)* I am being myself. *(She gets up and moves the chair back to its usual place)*

Frank   What's that?

Rita   What?

Frank   On your back.

Rita   *(Reaching up)* Oh – it's grass.

Frank   Grass?

Rita   Yeh, I got here early today. I started talking to some students down on the lawn. *(She sits in her usual chair)*

Frank   You were talking to students – down there?

Rita   *(Laughing)* Don't sound so surprised. I can talk now y'know, Frank.

Frank   I'm not surprised. Well! You used to be quite wary of them didn't you?

Rita   God knows why. For students they don't half come out with some rubbish y'know.

Frank	You're telling me?
Rita	I only got talking to them in the first place because as I was walking past I heard one of them sayin' as a novel he preferred *Lady Chatterley* to *Sons and Lovers*. I thought, I can keep walkin' and ignore it, or I can put him straight. So I put him straight. I walked over an' said, 'Excuse me but I couldn't help overhearin' the rubbish you were spoutin' about Lawrence.' Shoulda seen the faces on them, Frank. I said tryin' to compare *Chatterley* and *Sons and Lovers* is like tryin' to compare sparkling wine with champagne. The next thing is there's this heated discussion, with me right in the middle of it.
Frank	I thought you said the student claimed to 'prefer' *Chatterley*, as a novel.
Rita	He did.
Frank	So he wasn't actually suggesting that it was superior.
Rita	Not at first – but then he did. He walked right into it…
Frank	And so you finished him off, did you, Rita?
Rita	Frank, he was askin' for it. He was an idiot. His argument just crumbled. It wasn't just me – everyone else agreed with me.

Frank returns to reading the essay.

	There was this really mad one with them; I've only been talkin' to them for five minutes and he's inviting me to go abroad with them all. They're all goin' to the South of France in the Christmas holidays, slummin' it.
Frank	You can't go.
Rita	What?
Frank	You can't go – you've got your exams.
Rita	My exams are before Christmas.
Frank	Well – you've got your results to wait for…
Rita	Tch. I couldn't go anyway.
Frank	Why? *(He looks at her)*
Rita	It's all right for them. They can just jump into a bleedin' van an' go away. But I can't.

He returns to the essay.

	Tiger they call him, he's the mad one. His real name's Tyson but they call him Tiger.
Frank	*(Looking up)* Is there any point me going on with this? *(He points to the essay)*
Rita	What?
Frank	Is there much point in working towards an examination if you're going to fall in love and set off for the South of…
Rita	*(Shocked)* What! Fall in love? With who? My God, Frank, I've just been talkin' to some students. I've heard of match-making but this is ridiculous.
Frank	All right, but please stop burbling on about Mr Tyson.
Rita	I haven't been burbling on.

He returns to the essay.

	What's it like?
Frank	Oh – it – erm – wouldn't look out of place with these. *(He places it on top of a pile of other essays on his desk)*
Rita	Honest?
Frank	Dead honest.

Black out.

Frank exits.

USING EDUCATING RITA BY WILLY RUSSELL

To understand this play, you must explore:
- ♣ the way the relationship between Frank and Rita develops;
- ♣ the content of Rita's lessons;
- ♣ the different effects created by Russell's use of humour.

Make notes on these questions to ensure you have a thorough overview of the play:

1. How is Julia presented in the play?
2. How effective is the contrast between Rita and Julia?
3. How is Denny presented in the play?
4. How does he compare to Frank?
5. What is the impact of Frank's alcohol addiction? What does this add to his character?
6. How does Russell present different relationships?
7. How important is the setting of the play, the early 1980s?
8. How is Frank's poetry presented in the play? Why does Frank give Rita his poetry to read?
9. What is the effect of not seeing any other characters other than Frank and Rita?
10. What reasons does Rita give for wanting to study literature?
11. How are Trish and the other students presented? How does their presentation change?
12. What is the attitude of the senior members of the university towards Frank?
13. What do the students think of Frank? How does this differ to Rita's view of him?
14. How typical a student is Rita? How typical a teacher is Frank?

See PCM 3 for further advice on how to explore a play.

With guidance from your teacher, choose **one** of the following essay questions for your English and/or English Literature folder:

- ▭ Read the extract on PCM 11. How has Rita changed since she attended Summer School? How does this affect her relationship with Frank?
- ▭ 'All I've ever done is take from you. I've never given you anything.' How accurate is Rita's assessment of her relationship with Frank?

See PCM 4 for advice on writing essays.

Post–1914 drama

CONFUSIONS BY ALAN AYCKBOURN

This is a collection of five one-act plays that are interlinked by their themes and characters. Ayckbourn presents a range of relationships to assist his portrayal of complex human emotions, such as loneliness and hypocrisy.

In the extract below, from *Drinking Companion*, Harry is trying to persuade Paula to go back to his hotel room with him. However, she continually deflects his advances.

Harry	Ah well. Cheers. No, as I say, I never thought I'd be spending this evening with two gorgeous girls.
Bernice	You never know your luck, do you?
Harry	Quite right, Bernice, many a true word. Never know your luck. Well, how are we three going to spend this evening?
Bernice	Well, we're…
Harry	Now, now. Plenty of time. Enjoy your drink first, then we'll decide. The night is young, as they say. So are we. Well, in my case, young at heart. *(He laughs)*
Paula	I don't think we'll be wanting to do very much this evening, actually.
Harry	All right, fair enough. Let's stay here then. Fine by me. Have a bite of dinner later.
Bernice	Oh no.
Harry	It's very good, the restaurant here, you know.
Paula	Oh no.
Harry	On me. On me, I don't often have the pleasure.
Bernice	I don't think either of us are very hungry, thank you.
Harry	Oh, come on, you've got to eat, you've got to eat. Keep up your strength. No, seriously, I would consider it a great honour. A great honour. Besides, there's nothing worse than eating alone, is there? Be nice if, just for once — the life I lead, I seem to spend my life eating alone.
Paula	Well, when you're at home you don't…
Harry	Ah, well. On those occasions, on those rare occasions… Matter of fact, to be frank, I'm not often there. I mean, I don't want to start boring you by talking about myself particularly but, well — let's just say I'm not very often at home. Enough said? Enough said. Cheers. *(Pause)* I mean, don't get me wrong. My wife and I, we're not separated, anything like that. It's just — well, to be perfectly honest she's a lot happier if I'm not at home too much. You might say, we no longer see eye to eye. If you follow my meaning. She's got very strong views on certain matters and, er — well there you are. I mean, I'm — as I was saying only a minute ago to Paula here — I'm by nature — easy going. However, it takes all sorts as they say. It so happens my wife is one of those people who considers that these sorts of things cannot be forgiven or forgotten — ever. No matter. No matter how much you may talk to her or apologize to

her about it. She's not a woman to take sorry for an answer. So there you are. I live there. On occasions. That's about all. But it's not life. I don't call that life. *(Pause)* Anyway, enough of my problems. *(Pause)* The point is this, if my wife were sitting here now with us all, she would have no claim over me whatsoever. Nor, let's be perfectly honest, would I have on her. Washout. Finish. Waiter, we'll have the same again, please.

The waiter approaches.

Bernice	No, thank you very much.
Paula	No. Harry, Harry…
Harry	Waiter! Same again here.
Bernice	No, thank you very much, No more, waiter.
Harry	Waiter, we want three more of the same.
Paula	No, honestly, Harry…
Harry	Three more, waiter, we'll argue it out later.
Waiter	Three more, sir.

The waiter departs.

Bernice	I don't want any more
Harry	Come on, that's only your first.
Bernice	That's all I want.
Harry	You've got to catch up with me and Paula, for God's sake.
Bernice	I don't have to at all.
Paula	It's very kind of you.
Harry	Well, he's bringing them now, it's too late. You needn't worry, it's on me. On me. I mean, I'm not a big drinker either, you know. Don't get me wrong. I'm not hooked on it. I can go for weeks without a drink, you know, if I have to. Doesn't bother me in the least. But, for God's sake, if I get the chance of sitting here with two simply stunning-looking creatures the like of which I have never set eyes upon before, believe you me – well, I think it calls for a drink. I don't drink at home, you know. Never drink at home.
Bernice	You're never there.
Harry	I only drink socially. I only drink to be sociable. No, never been my problem, drinking. I've got other problems but drink's not one of them. Thank God. And I do very sincerely thank God. I won't go into my other problems, I don't want to shock you. *(He laughs)*

USING CONFUSIONS BY ALAN AYCKBOURN

To understand these plays you must explore:

♦ the way the separate plays are interlinked and the strengths and weaknesses of the one-act play format;
♦ Ayckbourn's attitude to relationships;
♦ the different ways Ayckbourn uses comedy.

Make notes on these questions to ensure you have a thorough overview of the plays:

1. In *Mother Figure*, what is so strange about Lucy's behaviour?
2. What does Lucy's behaviour reveal about the state of her marriage?
3. What effect does Lucy's behaviour have on the way Terry and Rosemary respond to each other?
4. How are Rosemary and Terry presented to the audience? How is their marriage portrayed?
5. In *Drinking Companion*, what is Paula's attitude to Harry?
6. What is the intended impact of Harry drinking so much?
7. What does Bernice contribute to the exchange?
8. Why does Harry fail to achieve his goal with Paula? How satisfying is this outcome for the audience and for Paula?
9. In *Between Mouthfuls*, what is the waiter's attitude to his guests?
10. How is Pearce presented? What is his relationship like with Mrs Pearce?
11. What does Martin and Polly's reaction reveal about their feelings towards Mr and Mrs Pearce?
12. How is Martin and Polly's relationship presented?
13. What is revealed towards the end of the play? How do the characters react to this news?
14. In *Gosforth's Fete*, how does Milly behave towards Mrs Pearce?
15. How is the vicar portrayed?
16. How does Gosforth's attitude change towards Milly and why?
17. How is Stewart presented?
18. What events occur while the speeches are being delivered?
19. What happens to Mrs Pearce and who is responsible?
20. In *A Talk in the Park*, how do each of the characters respond to each other?
21. Why is the final line of the play so significant?

See PCM 3 for further advice on how to explore a play.

With guidance from your teacher, choose **one** of the following essay questions for your English and/or English Literature folder:

▭ Read the extract on PCM 13. What does this exchange reveal about Harry's attitude towards his wife? How does his marriage compare to other relationships presented in the play?
▭ What are the *Confusions* in each of the plays? What impact do they have on the main characters and the people around them?

See PCM 4 for advice on writing essays.

Drama from different cultures and traditions

THE CRUCIBLE BY ARTHUR MILLER

The plot is based on the real events of the Salem witch trials in 1692. Rumours of black magic were spread rapidly by mass hysteria around the town of Salem in the American colonies. Many innocent townswomen were accused, tried, and hanged for the crime of witchcraft.

In the extract below, Elizabeth and John Proctor are discussing the forthcoming trial and the activities of Abigail Williams and Mary Warren. Elizabeth and John argue indirectly over John's affair with Abigail.

Act 2

Elizabeth	Mary Warren's there today.
Proctor	Why'd you let her? You heard me forbid her go to Salem any more!
Elizabeth	I couldn't stop her.
Proctor	*(Holding back a full condemnation of her)* It is a fault, it is a fault, Elizabeth – you're the mistress here. Not Mary Warren.
Elizabeth	She frightened all my strength away.
Proctor	How may that mouse frighten you, Elizabeth? You…
Elizabeth	It is a mouse no more. I forbid her go, and she raises up her chin like the daughter of a prince and says to me, 'I must go to Salem, Goody Proctor; I am an official of the court!'
Proctor	Court! What court?
Elizabeth	Aye, it is a proper court they have now. They've sent four judges out of Boston, she says, weighty magistrates of the General Court, and at the head sits the Deputy Governor of the Province.
Proctor	*(Astonished)* Why, she's mad.
Elizabeth	I would to God she were. There be fourteen people in the jail now, she says.

Proctor simply looks at her, unable to grasp it.

Elizabeth	And they'll be tried, and the court have power to hang them too, she says.
Proctor	*(Scoffing, but without conviction)* Ah, they'd never hang…
Elizabeth	The Deputy Governor promise hangin' if they'll not confess, John. The town's gone wild, I think. She speak of Abigail, and I thought she were a saint, to hear her. Abigail brings the other girls into the court, and where she walks the crowd will part like the sea for Israel. And folks are brought before them, and if they scream and howl and fall to the floor – the person's clapped in the jail for bewitchin' them.
Proctor	*(Wide-eyed)* Oh, it is a black mischief.
Elizabeth	I think you must go to Salem, John. *(He turns to her.)* I think it. You must tell them it is a fraud.
Proctor	*(Thinking beyond this)* Aye, it is, it is surely.
Elizabeth	Let you go to Ezekiel Cheever – he knows you well. And tell him what she said to you last week in her uncle's house. She said it had naught to do with witchcraft, did she not?
Proctor	*(In thought)* Aye, she did, she did. *(Now, a pause.)*

Elizabeth	*(Quietly, fearing to anger him by prodding)* God forbid you keep that from the court, John. I think they must be told.
Proctor	*(Quietly, struggling with his thought)* Aye, they must, they must. It is a wonder they do believe her.
Elizabeth	I would go to Salem now, John – let you go tonight.
Proctor	I'll think on it.
Elizabeth	*(With her courage now)* You cannot keep it, John.
Proctor	*(Angering)* I know I cannot keep it. I say I will think on it!
Elizabeth	*(Hurt, and very coldly)* Good, then, let you think on it. *(She stands and starts to walk out of the room.)*
Proctor	I am only wondering how I may prove what she told me, Elizabeth. If the girl's a saint now, I think it is not easy to prove she's a fraud, and the town gone so silly. She told it to me in a room alone – I have no proof for it.
Elizabeth	You were alone with her?
Proctor	*(Stubbornly)* For a moment alone, aye.
Elizabeth	Why, then, it is not as you told me.
Proctor	*(His anger rising)* For a moment, I say. The others come in soon after.
Elizabeth	*(Quietly – she has suddenly lost all faith in him)* Do as you wish, then. *(She starts to turn.)*
Proctor	Woman. *(She turns to him with suspicion)* I'll not have your suspicion any more.
Elizabeth	*(A little loftily)* I have no...
Proctor	I'll not have it!
Elizabeth	Then let you not earn it.
Proctor	*(With a violent undertone)* You doubt me yet?
Elizabeth	*(With a smile, to keep her dignity)* John, if it were not Abigail that you must go to hurt, would you falter now? I think not.
Proctor	Now look you...
Elizabeth	I see what I see, John.
Proctor	*(With solemn warning)* You will not judge me more, Elizabeth. I have good reason to think before I charge fraud on Abigail, and I will think on it. Let you look to your own improvement before you go to judge your husband any more. I have forgot Abigail, and...
Elizabeth	And I.
Proctor	Spare me! You forget nothin' and forgive nothin'. Learn charity, woman. I have gone tiptoe in this house all seven month since she is gone. I have not moved from there to there without I think to please you, and still an everlasting funeral marched round your heart. I cannot speak but I am doubted, every moment judged for lies, as though I come into a court when I come into this house!
Elizabeth	John, you are not open with me. You saw her with a crowd, you said. Now you...
Proctor	I'll plead my honesty no more, Elizabeth.
Elizabeth	*(Now she would justify herself)* John, I am only...
Proctor	No more! I should have roared you down when first you told me your suspicion. But I wilted, and, like a Christian, I confessed. Confessed! Some dream I had must have mistaken you for God that day. But you're not, you're not, and let you remember it! Let you look sometimes for the goodness in me, and judge me not.
Elizabeth	I do not judge you. The magistrate sits in your heart that judges you. I never thought you but a good man, John – *(With a smile)* – only somewhat bewildered.
Proctor	Oh, Elizabeth, your justice would freeze beer!

USING THE CRUCIBLE BY ARTHUR MILLER

To understand this play, you must explore:

♣ the power of, and consequences of, mass hysteria;
♣ the roles of both religion and the Devil in Salem;
♣ the inadequacies of the justice system, including the 'eyewitness' accounts of events.

Make notes on these questions to ensure you have a thorough overview of the play:

1. What is Parris' main priority in Act 1?
2. What are some of the reasons why people are visiting Parris' house?
3. What are Betty Parris' reported symptoms?
4. What does Abigail claim she and the other girls were doing in the forest? What were they actually doing?
5. What accusations are made against Parris during the course of the play?
6. What is the role of Reverend Hale in the play?
7. What is the role of Rebecca Nurse in the play?
8. What kind of person is Ezekiel Cheever?
9. How is Tituba portrayed? How do the other characters respond to her
10. What is the relationship like between John and Elizabeth Proctor?
11. What is the relationship like between Thomas and Ann Putnam? What is their relationship like with other members of the society?
12. Why do the people in Salem believe the girls are witches?
13. How fair is their trial?
14. How is Mary Warren portrayed? How do other characters respond to her?
15. How does Miller use irony in the play?

See PCM 3 for further advice on how to explore a play.

With guidance from your teacher, choose **one** of the following essay questions for your English and/or English Literature folder:

▪ Read the extract on PCM 15. How is Elizabeth Proctor portrayed in this exchange and elsewhere in the play? How does she differ from Abigail Williams?
▪ Who is most responsible for the consequences of John Proctor's sexual encounter with Abigail Williams?

See PCM 4 for advice on writing essays.

Drama from different cultures and traditions

THE CAUCASIAN CHALK CIRCLE BY BERTOLT BRECHT

Grusha, a servant girl, rescues Michael, the abandoned baby son of the Governor, and she flees with him to the mountains. Meanwhile, the Governor's wife, Michael's real mother, desperately wants to have her child back. The Judge sets up the Chalk Circle as a test of which of these two women should be Michael's mother.

In the extract below, the Governor's wife is being urged to leave their house because of the peasants' revolt. However, she is reluctant to leave without her most precious belongings and most expensive dresses. She shows little concern for her son and refuses to believe that the peasants will harm her.

Scene 2

Simon Chachava leaps to attention and goes off. Two servants crawl in from the gateway, loaded down with heavy trunks. Behind them, supported by her women, stumbles Natella Abashvili. She is followed by another woman carrying Michael.

Governor's wife As usual, nobody's paying the slightest attention. I hardly know if I'm standing on my head or my feet. Where's Michael? Don't hold him so clumsily! Pile the trunks on to the carriage! Shalva, is there any word from the Governor?

Adjutant *(Shaking his head)* You must get away at once.

Governor's wife Is there any news from the town?

Adjutant No. So far all is quiet. But there isn't a minute to lose. There's not enough room for the trunks on the carriage. Please pick out what you need.

Exit the Adjutant quickly.

Governor's wife Only essentials! Quick, open the trunks. I'll tell you what I've got to have.

The trunks are lowered and opened.

Governor's wife *(Pointing at some brocade dresses)* That green one! And of course that one with the fur trimming. Where are the doctors? I'm getting this terrible migraine again. It always starts in the temples. This one with the little pearl buttons…*(Enter Grusha)* You're taking your time, eh? Go and get the hot water bottles at once!

Grusha runs off, and returns with hot water bottles. The Governor's wife orders her about by signs.

Governor's wife *(Watching a young woman attendant)* Don't tear the sleeve!

Young woman I promise you, madam, no harm has come to the dress.

Governor's wife	Because I caught you. I've been watching you for a long time. Nothing in your head but making eyes at the Adjutant. I'll kill you, you bitch! *(She beats her)*
Adjutant	*(Returning)* I must ask you to make haste, Natella Abashvili. They are fighting in the town.

Exit the Adjutant.

Governor's wife	*(Letting go of the young woman)* My God, do you think they'll do something to me? Why should they? *(All are silent. She herself begins to rummage in the trunks)* Where's my brocade jacket? Help me! What about Michael? Is he asleep?
Nurse	Yes, madam.
Governor's wife	Then put him down a moment and go and fetch my little morocco slippers from the bedchamber. I need them to go with the green dress. *(The nurse puts down the child and goes off. To the young woman)* Don't stand around, you! *(The young woman runs off)* Stay here, or I'll have you flogged! Just look at the way these things have been packed! No love! No understanding! If one doesn't give every order oneself... At such moments one realizes what one's servants are like! Masha! *(She gives her an order with a wave of the hand)* You all gorge yourselves, but never a sign of gratitude! I won't forget this.
Adjutant	*(Very excited)* Natella, you must leave at once! Orbeliani, Judge of the Supreme Court, has just been hanged! The carpet weavers are in revolt!
Governor's wife	Why? I must have the silver dress – it cost 1,000 piastres. And that one there, and all my furs. And where's the wine-coloured dress?
Adjutant	*(Trying to pull her away)* Riots have broken out in the outer town! We've got to leave this minute! *(A servant runs off)* Where's the child?
Governor's wife	*(To the nurse)* Maro, get the child ready! Where are you?
Adjutant	*(Leaving)* We'll probably have to do without the carriage. And ride.

The Governor's wife still rummages among her dresses, throws some on to the heap to go with her, then takes them off again. Drums are heard. The sky begins to redden.

Governor's wife	*(Rummaging desperately)* I can't find that wine-coloured dress. *(Shrugging her shoulders, to the second woman)* Take the whole heap and carry it to the carriage. Why hasn't Maro come back? Have you all gone off your heads? I told you it's right at the bottom.
Adjutant	*(Returning)* Quick! Quick!
Governor's wife	*(To the second woman)* Run! Just throw them into the carriage!
Adjutant	We're not going by carriage. Come at once or I'll ride off on my own!
Governor's wife	Maro! Bring the child! *(To the second woman)* Go and look, Masha. No, first take the dresses to the carriage. It's all nonsense, I wouldn't dream of riding! *(Turning round, she sees the fire-reddened sky and starts back in horror)* Fire! *(She rushes off, followed by the Adjutant. The second woman, shaking her head, follows with a heap of dresses.)*

USING THE CAUCASIAN CHALK CIRCLE BY BERTOLT BRECHT

To understand this play, you must explore:
- ♠ the significance of the 'Chalk Circle';
- ♠ the moral – 'give resources to those best able to use them';
- ♠ the way the two units of the play are united by this moral.

Make notes on these questions to ensure you have a thorough overview of the play:

1. What is the significance of the dispute between the goat-breeders and the fruit-farmers?
2. How does the way this dispute is resolved reflect the moral of the play?
3. What is the role of Grusha in the play?
4. How important is the relationship between Grusha and Simon, a soldier?
5. What prompts Grusha to save Michael, the Governor's son?
6. What is the role of the folk-singer in the play?
7. What is the significance of the revolt of the peasants against the Governor?
8. Why is Grusha thrown out of the caravansary?
9. Grusha leaves Michael with a peasant woman. What does the exchange between Grusha and this peasant woman reveal about Grusha's character?
10. What do the Ironshirts contribute to the dramatic action of the play?
11. How does Grusha compare to Natella Abashvili, the Governor's wife?
12. How does Azdak become Judge? How good a Judge is he?
13. How satisfying is the ending of the play?

See PCM 3 for further advice on how to explore a play.

With guidance from your teacher, choose **one** of the following essay questions for your English and/or English Literature folder:

- ▬ Read the extract on PCM 17. How is the governor's wife, Natella Abashvili, portrayed in this exchange? How does this affect the audience's sympathy for her in the final scene?
- ▬ What is Azdak's role in the play? How does his behaviour change?

See PCM 4 for advice on writing essays.

Drama with Welsh relevance

ACT ONE WALES BY VARIOUS AUTHORS

These are thirteen variations on the one-act play, each of which is set in Wales and/or offers a perspective on Welsh life. The plays cover a broad range of themes and their characters provoke powerful responses from the audience, either by their similarities to us, their heartfelt confrontations or by their controversial points of view.

In the extract below from *Sailing to America* by Duncan Bush, two women are lying in adjacent hospital beds in a ward for the terminally ill. They are discussing their own situation and the situation of others, both currently and from when they were younger.

Josie   I wonder who they'll put in there. *(Pause)* Well, it won't be Hedy Lamarr. *(Pause)* I don't suppose it'll be empty long. There's people crying out for beds. Like Sister always says, you'll have to get better quicker, we need the beds. *(Pause)* Die quicker, she means. That's how it usually turns out. *(Pause)* I expect they'll put somebody in there by tonight. *(Pause)* I hope it's someone a bit younger. They're all so old and gaga in this ward. *(Pause)* Someone with a bit of life in them. A bit of personality. Brighten the place up a bit.

Evelyn   Don't say that. Don't wish it on the young. Let them live their lives out first. *(Josie looks at the empty bed.)*

Josie   Not another one like her was all I meant. *(Pause)* I know she couldn't help it. And far be it from me to speak ill of the departed, wherever she is now. But she was hardly the bleeding highspot of the evening, was she? *(Pause)* It makes you ill sometimes, it do, just to see some of the cases they got here. *(Pause)* It's like that film on the telly the other afternoon. Where he's in prison for a murder he didn't do. On the word of that bitch. She's as good as laughing at him in the dock as they drag him away. And that metal door bangs shut on him, and you know he knows that's it. It's like a nightmare to him. But it's not. It's really happening. And he's there for the rest of his days. *(Pause)* Sometimes that's how I feel. Like they got the wrong person. Like, what did I ever do to anybody to deserve to end up here? *(Pause)* No wonder nobody's keen on visiting. *(Silence)* You know, once they get like that. *(Pause)* I know it's a terrible thing to say, but it was a relief when she went. When you realized it had stopped, you couldn't hear her no more. *(Pause)* I don't think I could have stood another night of lying here and listening to her. That terrible snore or dragging rattle or whatever it was, like every breath she managed to draw in was going to be the last. Only, it went on. All day, all night.

Evelyn   I blame the food.

Josie   Eh?

Evelyn   It's not just the being bedridden. I was bedridden at home. I blame the food. *(Pause)* I'm not saying it's bad food, or badly cooked. And they keep those kitchens spotless. *(Pause)* They give you too much of it. Three big meals a day. Like you was a navvy or something. When, in here, you didn't ought to eat more than a cage bird strictly speaking. If they gave you less you'd feel better for it, don't you think?

You're not using it up, are you, as energy? Not in here.

Josie   Christ, meals are the only thing you got to look forward to. *(Pause)* Not that it's all that marvellous, the food. But it's something to do three times a day. You know, managing the tray. *(Pause)* Try cutting down. Or going vegetarian. After a day or two you'll probably find you want to go. And at least you won't feel so heavy.

Evelyn   Heavy? Sometimes I feel so light it's only the sheets keep me from floating off. *(Silence, in which Josie closes her eyes as if for a doze.)*

Josie   It's only when you shut your eyes that you hear all the noises. *(Silence. Evelyn closes her eyes too.)* All the clanks and footsteps and trolleys out in the corridor. And that hum, it must be the central heating, and the systems. *(Pause)* It never stops, that hum. *(Pause)* I say hum. It's worse than a hum. It's more like a big wheel grinding round and round. Or some massive big machine vibrating somewhere a long way away. That's what a day is, here: the noise of that machine going. *(Pause)* You can lie here at night for hours, just listening to it. No, trying to listen to it. But hearing it, no matter what. *(Pause)* It's the same if you try shutting your eyes for a nap. You can lie here for hours and not notice it, that noise. But soon as you shut your eyes to go to sleep it's back. *(Pause)* It's like you're going somewhere on a ship, the noise of the engine room. *(Pause)* Sometimes even when I'm asleep I hear it. *(Pause)* I can feel the movement under me. The ocean. And then I know it is a ship. And it's taking me somewhere. It's like the whole hospital, all those wings and floors lit up, and me on my bed in it, is steaming off into the dark. Like a big transatlantic liner sailing off to America. *(Pause)* And I think, this is it, I've always wanted to see America. *(Pause)* And I know this is a trip I won't wake up on. *(Pause)* Then I do. *(Pause. Josie opens her eyes and stares upwards.)* And you open your eyes, it's the middle of the night, and you're in the ward and you got that bleeding ceiling light still on. *(Silence)*

Evelyn   Like in 'Casablanca'. They're out on the deck. You can see the rail and the sea behind them with the moonlight on it. And Paul Muni's in a white dinner jacket with a dickie-bow. And Hedy Lamarr's got a shawl on, because it's cooler at night. *(Pause)* And Paul Muni puts two cigarettes in his mouth and lights them. And he has to shield the match because of the breeze off the sea. And he takes one of the cigarettes out of his mouth and puts it in hers.

Josie   Paul Muni? Was he in that?

Evelyn   And you know that's not really the sea behind them. And they're not really on the deck of a ship. It's just a bit of rail, with some kind of film on a screen, or whatever it is they use, to show that twinkly shimmery look of the sea. *(Pause)* It's like in the South seas or somewhere. You know, with the moon on it, and the night so clear. *(Pause)* And you can see it's not real. It's just a background. But it always used to make me think, I'd love to be there. To be out on deck. With the moonlight shining on the sea like that, right out to the horizon. And them not even noticing it because they only had eyes for each other. *(Pause)* And then they'd show you just her face as he was going to kiss her. And she smiles as she waits for him to. And even her eyes and teeth and hair and jewellery would have that soft twinkle, like the sea.

USING ACT ONE WALES BY VARIOUS AUTHORS

To understand these plays, you must explore:
- ♣ the restrictions of the one-act-play format;
- ♣ the use of Wales as a setting for each of the plays;
- ♣ the sharp focus on character in each of the plays.

Make notes on these questions to ensure you have a thorough overview of the plays;

1. What is the effect of using a narrator in the plays?
2. What is the effect of using faceless voices in the plays?
3. What is the effect of only using two characters in the plays? How does this affect the audience's interpretation of events?
4. How do the plays portray family life?
5. How do the plays describe Wales?
6. What is revealed in the plays about Welsh culture?
7. How do the plays portray different reactions to everyday situations?
8. What is revealed about Welsh history?
9. How do the playwrights explore different human emotions?
10. How do the playwrights create intense and believable emotions in only thirty minutes?
11. What is the effect of using dialect and slang in the plays? Why do some playwrights choose not to use dialect in their plays?
12. How do the playwrights use irony and/or humour in their plays?
13. How do the playwrights manipulate different time scales in their plays? What effect does this have on the events of the plays?

See PCM 3 for further advice on how to explore a play.

With guidance from your teacher, choose **one** of the following essay questions for your English and/or English Literature folder:

▬ Read the extract on PCM 19. What do these two ladies reveal about themselves? How do these characters compare to other women portrayed in the *Act One Wales* plays?

▬ Select any two of the *Act One Wales* plays and explain how they entertain and satisfy the audience.

See PCM 4 for advice on writing essays.

Drama with Welsh relevance

ON THE ROAD AGAIN, THE BEST YEARS OF OUR LIVES, CRADLE TO THE GRAVE
BY LAURENCE ALLAN

These three plays explore different aspects of life in Wales. The plays are both humorous and touching, and present views of Wales that are simultaneously familiar and unpredictable.

In the extract below from *Cradle to the Grave*, the construction workers Animal and Christian are preparing to demolish the local hospital. Unknown to them, a patient, Nye Bevan, is lying in the hospital behind a curtain. (Nye Bevan was a Labour minister from South Wales who was Minister of Health when the National Health Service was started in 1948.)

(We hear 'Everything Must Go' – The Manics. Two people appear, Christian and Animal, dressed in overalls, industrial masks and hard hats. One is wielding a power saw, the other a power drill. One is carrying a ghetto blaster.)

Christian   Where do we start?

Animal   Anywhere.

Christian   What do we do?

Animal   Take it out.

Christian   Take what out?

Animal   Everything.

Christian   Everything?

Animal   Trust me.

Christian   I trust you.

Animal   Everything must go.

Christian   Everything must go.

(They start the machines up.)

Animal   *(Starts to sing)* 'And if you need an explanation, then everything must go…'

Christian   *(Joining in)* 'And I hope that you can forgive us, but everything must go…'

(They advance – a sharp suited man walks in – Mendleson – he watches them)

Mendleson   Having fun?

(They see him and switch off)

Animal   Mister Mendleson.

Mendleson	What is all this about?
Animal	It's a song.
Christian	Nihilistic denial of post modernism.
Animal	No it's not.
Mendleson	I am not talking about — *(He stops himself)* What were your instructions?
Animal	Rip it out.
Christian	Everything must go.
Mendleson	Everything must — you're new to us, aren't you? Well your colleague here, Mr —
Animal	Animal
Mendleson	Animal has been here for over six — I refuse to call you Animal. I refuse to believe that anyone would want to call you Animal.
Animal	It's after that drummer in The Muppets.
Christian	You play the drums?
Animal	No.
Mendleson	I don't want to know any more. And if you tell me your name is Kermit because you look nothing like a frog —
Christian	Christian. My name's Christian.
Mendleson	Good. I can deal with that. That's the sort of name that rests easily on a salvage worker. That's salvage, Animal, note the extra consonant from the word that you're mistaking it for.
Animal	Even drummers can spell, Mister Mendleson.
Mendleson	But you're not a — no, no, we'll leave that one there. Do you know what you're doing? Exactly.
Animal	We're gutting the place.
Mendleson	Gutting. Gutting. This place that you're 'gutting' is an architectural timepiece, a veritable goldmine of Victorian artefacts. I do not want you 'gutting' the b*******s out of it.
Animal	I do know the difference between artefacts and b*******s, Mister Mendleson.
Mendleson	I don't think you know the difference between artefacts and artex.
Animal	Yeah, I do. Artefact's got a whole bunch of different consonants in it.
Mendleson	Right. OK. Fine. We've had the comedy, now let's survey the damage, shall we? For a start, where've you put the sign?
Christian	What sign?
Mendleson	Cardiff City People's hospital? Some fine mid-century wrought iron work?

Animal	There was no sign.
Christian	We weren't sure we were in the right place.
Mendleson	God help us. It's just as well Llandaff Cathedral is signposted, you'd have ended up gutting that.
Animal	Perhaps someone nicked it.
Mendleson	There's been round the clock security.
Christian	Perhaps they nicked it.
Animal	Or one of them nurses. As a memento.
Mendleson	You think a nurse would actually – right, fine, let's leave that, shall we? Get down to some real work.
Animal	Suits me, Mister Mendleson.
Christian	Yeah, suits us.
Mendleson	Right. We'll make a start in Maternity.
Animal	What are we going to find there?
Christian	Edwardian afterbirth?
Animal	Victorian foetus in a jar.
Mendleson	I really have employed a pair of muppets, haven't I?
Animal	No. *(Silence, then he starts to sing)* 'It's time to put on makeup, it's time to start the show...'
Mendleson	In the Labour Ward surrounding what I believe they now call the Delivery Suite, there is some intricate and delicate friezework. I would like it taken down and removed with absolute care, love and attention. *(Exits)*
Animal	Love and attention.
Christian	Care, love and attention.

(They start up the machines. They move towards the curtains around Bevan's bed. Bevan comes to, screams.)

Animal	What the hell is he doing here?
Christian	Having a baby?
Animal	He shouldn't be here. He shouldn't be here, no way.
Christian	Perhaps we shouldn't.
Animal	Mister Mendleson! Mister Mendleson!

(They leave.)

USING ON THE ROAD AGAIN, THE BEST YEARS OF OUR LIVES, CRADLE TO THE GRAVE BY LAURENCE ALLAN

To understand these plays, you must explore:

♣ the use of humour to enhance the plot of each play;
♣ the portrayal of Welsh people;
♣ the constraints of each of the settings for the plays.

Make notes on these questions to ensure you have a thorough overview of the plays:

1. In *On the Road Again*, what kind of men are Rich and Beefy?
2. What is the effect of Rich's disjointed behaviour at the beginning of the play?
3. How similar or different are Rich and Beefy?
4. How is their accommodation described?
5. What is the impact of the eviction notice on the relationship between Rich and Beefy?
6. What is the impact of their discussion about what they could have been?
7. In *The Best Years of Our Lives*, what is the impact of the coal mine closing?
8. How is the character of Eddie portrayed?
9. How does Neil feel about his future?
10. What images of neighbourliness does Neil present? How does this relate to his relationship with Fiona and Rob?
11. What is the *'Heritage Trail'*? What do the characters each think of this idea?
12. Why does Clem go on a hunger strike? How do the other characters react to this?
13. Why does Glen *'turn Japanese'*?
14. How does the plan to kidnap the Secretary of State for Wales develop?
15. In *Cradle to the Grave*, what comment is Allan making about the state of the NHS in this play?
16. How does Allan use irony?
17. What impressions does the audience get of Bevan?
18. How are Animal and Christian portrayed? What do they contribute to the play?
19. What is the effect of Dr Lee being drunk?
20. What is the effect of Bevan's confusion on the audience?
21. Is the audience meant to assume that this is a typical NHS hospital? Explain your answer.
22. What is the effect of the fast pace of the action?

See PCM 3 for further advice on how to explore a play.

Task

With guidance from your teacher, choose one of the following essay questions for your English and/or English Literature folder:

▬ Read the extract on PCM 21. How does Allan create humour in this scene? What are the different uses of humour in these plays?

▬ What comments about Wales and its people does Allan make in these plays?

See PCM 4 for advice on writing essays.

Open Writing

Notes for teachers

The English specification
        2004 and beyond
        Open Writing 'triplets'
Planning considerations – organizing Open Writing work
        Links with Open Writing in Paper 1
        Drafting policy
        Submitting poetry for Open Writing coursework
        Monitoring Open Writing
        Notes on using the photocopy masters (PCMs)

Photocopy masters (PCMs)

GENERAL

TASK SHEETS

Notes for teachers

The English specification

2004 and beyond

For 2004 and beyond, students must have one piece of 'Open' Writing in their English coursework folders. 'Open' Writing will take the form of writing **either** to *inform, explain, describe* **or** to *explore, imagine, entertain*. In practice, this will most often be a piece of personal, reflective, or descriptive writing, a narrative, or a drama script.

Open Writing 'triplets' of purposes

- *Inform, explain, describe* – in this section, this 'triplet' is covered through autobiographical writing and travel writing.
- *Explore, imagine, entertain* – in this section, this 'triplet' is covered through narrative fiction writing and play-script writing.

In reality, these triplets will generally be subsumed and overlapped by the demands of a given task, and the potential of any genuinely 'open' response.

Planning considerations – organizing Open Writing work

Experience shows that students thrive when they are invited to write in a genuinely open way, without the constraining demands of a specific literary text. Literature works best as a stimulus for writing on a loosely thematic level, or as a model of narrative and descriptive style and structure. Empathy tasks, based on the study of characters in a literary text, can produce excellent imaginative writing, but constrain students to some degree from a fully open response. In other words, empathy tasks on literature are valid, but not necessarily successful.

Links with Open Writing in Paper 1

Candidates are required to complete a descriptive writing task **and** a narrative writing task on GCSE English Paper 1 (Section B). GCSE English coursework should offer regular opportunities to practise Open Writing skills, rather than a single chance to fill the slot in the coursework folder. This practice will help students when they come to sit the examination.

The four broad task areas dealt with in this section are closely related to the needs of Section B on Paper 1. It is recommended that good coursework practice should inform the approach to examination tasks, rather than the reverse. In other words, do not transfer timed responses to examination questions directly to the coursework folders.

One successful way of linking coursework to preparation for the examination is to set an exam-writing task as a timed classroom test, then to require students to develop their response through a drafting process into a rather longer and better considered coursework piece. The drafting process, if managed by teachers in an enlightened way, enhances students' confidence and independence in writing, which will bear fruit in the examination.

Drafting policy

'Clean copies' of students' writing are not allowed in coursework. Students should be guided both during and after the preparation of a first draft of a piece of work, but it is neither acceptable, nor sensible, to correct all errors and then instruct a student to make a clean copy. The final piece should be recognizably the student's own work, reflecting his or her proofreading skills, the honing of which should pay dividends in Paper 1 and Paper 2 when the student obviously has to write independently and under pressure of time.

Whatever the precise details of a department's policy on drafting, it is very important that all colleagues support the policy.

Submitting poetry for Open Writing coursework

Traditionally, few students submit their own poetry for GCSE, but individuals should not be discouraged from doing so, provided they understand that it must be written with the rigour that would be evident in any prose writing. The structure and development of a poem are critical to its credibility as a coursework submission – it should have some shape. Pragmatically, moderators will expect some parity of achievement between poetry and prose writing at any mark point, and all interested parties will understand the fairness of that. There may be more expectation of a drafting process as visible evidence. A small collection of poems (3 or 4 only) might also confirm the student's ongoing serious interest in writing poetry.

Monitoring Open Writing

By its very nature, Open Writing is difficult for a moderator to validate and, occasionally, teachers represent little of the teaching and monitoring process as support for the assessment made and the mark awarded. If most of the writing is to be done outside the classroom, teachers should engage as fully as possible in the drafting process, through dialogue with each student. Where the teacher, with a light touch, has been involved in the creative process, he or she can supportively report the student's engagement in the task to the moderator.

Notes on using the photocopy masters (PCMs)

PCMs 1-5 provide general information for students, which can be used at an individual teacher's discretion. PCM 1 explains the position of Open Writing within the English course and PCM 2 explains the grading structure and relevant assessment criteria for students. PCM 3 focuses upon spelling, punctuation, and grammar. In addition, spelling, punctuation, and grammar are given full and detailed consideration in the GCSE textbook that accompanies this coursework file. PCM 4 gives students the opportunity to practise editing and proofreading a specimen piece of coursework before they begin work on their own pieces. PCM 5 (a and b) takes this forward and relates the need for proofreading directly with assessment and grading.

The remainder of this section comprises task-centred work. For each of the four Open Writing tasks (on PCMs 9, 12, 16, and 19), two exemplar pieces of writing have been offered on preceding PCMs as stimuli for discussion. All of the exemplar pieces have been written by GCSE students and stand, therefore, as fairly realistic models of achievement for

candidates across the ability range. (These exemplar pieces have been slightly amended for publication where necessary.)

On PCMs 6 and 13, there are a number of questions for students to use as they evaluate both the exemplar pieces and their own work arising from the task sheets. It is assumed that established texts and extracts are also available for students, and that teachers will link features of detailed study and wider reading to the needs of each task. The task sheets themselves try to reflect the spirit of Open Writing, i.e. that it offers scope for personal expression.

Where Open Writing fits into your course

Open Writing is writing to

inform, explain, describe
or to
explore, imagine, entertain.

It includes personal, reflective, and descriptive writing. It also includes narrative (fictional) writing, drama scripts, and (own) poetry.

You will be assessed on your skill with plot, mood, setting, atmosphere, and characterization; and your ability to:

♣ communicate clearly and imaginatively
♣ use and adapt forms for different readers and purposes
♣ organize ideas into sentences, paragraphs, and whole texts
♣ use a range of sentence structures effectively
♣ use a wide vocabulary
♣ use the grammar of standard English
♣ use accurate spelling
♣ use accurate punctuation
♣ present work neatly and clearly

In **English coursework**:

♣ **one** piece of Open Writing will be submitted for final assessment. It will take the form of writing to *inform, explain, describe* **or** to *explore, imagine, entertain.*

In **English Paper 1**:

♣ there will be **two** imaginative (or Open) Writing tasks. The first will ask for a piece of writing to *inform, explain, describe.* The second will offer opportunities for a variety of approaches in writing to *explore, imagine, entertain.*

Therefore, be as independent as you can when drafting, editing, and proofreading your coursework, so that you can cope on your own in the examination.

Making the grade in Open Writing coursework

G > F > E

- Students at grade 'E' can attempt a range of writing styles. They have some control of, for example, plot, mood, setting, atmosphere, and characterization. There is some awareness of purpose and audience. The subject matter is organized logically.
- They have some control of grammar and generally use vocabulary that is appropriate to tasks. They generally spell common words correctly. There is some control and variety of sentence structures. There is some organization and punctuation control.

E > D > C

- Students at grade 'C' are competent in a range of writing styles. They can consciously construct, for example, plot, mood, setting, atmosphere, and characterization, using detail, control, and shape. There is a sense of purpose and audience. The subject matter is coherently and logically organized, and there is some use of devices for particular effects.
- Their grammar is generally appropriate and there is some variety in their vocabulary, which is mostly spelled correctly. They control tenses, agreements, punctuation, and a variety of sentence structures. Their organization is sound.

C > B > A > A*

- Students at grade 'A*' are assured and highly competent in a range of writing styles. They are skilful in, for example, creating plot, setting, atmosphere, mood, and characterization. There is consistent awareness of purpose and chosen audience. Complex subject matter is organized and presented coherently. There is effective use of devices for particular effects.
- They can use a wide range of grammar and they have a wide vocabulary, appropriately used, which they spell correctly. They construct complex sentences accurately. They have secure control of tenses, agreements, and connectives. They have secure control of punctuation. Their sentences and paragraphs are coherently linked.

Spelling, punctuation, and grammar

Look closely at either:

♣ one of your own pieces of work
   or
♣ one of the student examples from this section.

Identify examples of each of the following:

Spelling

♣ homophones (e.g. there and their)
♣ vowel choices (e.g. rec<u>ei</u>ve, bec<u>au</u>se)
♣ double consonants (e.g. sho<u>pp</u>ing)
♣ irregular plurals (e.g. part<u>ies</u>)
♣ word endings (e.g. enjoy<u>ed</u>)
♣ silent letters (e.g. <u>k</u>nife)
♣ polysyllabic (e.g. int<u>e</u>rest – 3 syllables not 2)

Punctuation

♣ full stops
♣ capital letters
♣ question marks
♣ apostrophes
♣ commas
♣ exclamation marks
♣ speech marks
♣ semi-colons
♣ colons
♣ brackets
♣ dashes

Grammar

♣ verb tenses (e.g. He has <u>forgotten</u> his wallet)
♣ correct use of pronouns (e.g. He and I have...)
♣ correctly formed verbs (e.g. <u>dug</u> not digged)
♣ subject-verb agreements (e.g. We were, I was)
♣ comparatives and superlatives (e.g. <u>bigger</u> than, big<u>gest</u>)

Drafting and proofreading

Many pieces of autobiographical writing for coursework start life like the piece below by Mark. Like so many other pieces of writing at GCSE, this has grade 'C' (and above) potential, but fails to achieve it for a number of reasons. The piece is obviously too short but it is not a case of Mark needing to return to the ending to add some more. Instead, he should engage again with his memory of the experience and expand selectively the details of each paragraph.

Task

1. How could Mark improve the quality of the action and description?
   * Think of at least three questions that you could ask Mark as prompts for him to improve the content.
2. How could Mark improve his use of language?
   * Work through the text (as Mark should have done!), correcting spelling, punctuation, and grammar.
   * Add or change words and/or phrases to improve his vocabulary and style.

I am a member of air cadets. last year I went on a camp to the Brecon Beacons with them. We stayed in a field next to some woods. I was the most senior cadet in our flight (group) so I was in charge of about 10-15 people. This one night we had an exersice whereby we were given our mission and we had to run off into the woods.

At first the weather was quite reasonable, but as the night progressed it started to rain and got quite cold.

Part of our mission was to go back to our campsite where we had to find some object but the opposing team were there and their misson was to stop us. We had two girls in our team who didn't like the Idea of this so they waited behind.

We were gone for 10 minutes because we got caught by the other team. So we went back into the woods looking for theese girls but they decided to move from the place that we left them, to a deeper part of the woods. we found them and the one girl said she was cold so we said we would take her back, then she fainted.

We all took our coats of and put them over her to keep her warm. Two of the cadets run off to get help from the staff. Nobody knew what was going on. Everything seemed to go on for hours. The girl was taken to hospital and was treated with hypothermia. She was alright, she came back on the camp the next day.

The whole incident seemed to last hours but it was only a couple of minutes.

NOTE:

You should seek general help from your teacher in finding and curing weaknesses in your use of language, but you should also get into the habit of proofreading your own work. You need to become a fully independent writer by the time you sit your GCSE exams. If your teacher does correct your coursework in detail, he or she must declare this to the Coursework Moderator.

WJEC COURSEWORK GUIDE   Open Writing

Sample Open Writing piece (assessment)

The following piece of autobiographical writing by Rhys Elsworth has not, unlike the writing elsewhere in this section, been corrected word for word. It has a lot of high-grade qualities but the final mark or grade would be compromised by the errors and lapses of style which it contains. It is each student's responsibility to edit and proofread his or her own coursework.

Read this piece through and identify all the weaknesses that need to be addressed by the writer.

I attended Bedwas Infants School after I had been to a nursery held in the local church. During my first day at school at break time, I met a friend who was almost forgotten from the nursery. His name was Alex Okill, he was taller than me at that time, and very pale faced. He wore a green coat over our royal blue uniforms. The weather was intensely cold, and every morning my mother would say: "Jack Frost has been again." I've never quite understood that saying. Anyway, everything was really cold and the sky was a cloudless marine blue. The worn grey concrete of the playground wielded danger, as it was slippery with the covering of winter frost.

After several weeks of being in school me and Alex got to know each other a little better and we met another friend from the nursery, Craig. He was shorter than me and fair blonde hair that was cut in the same style a Alex's. A bowl cut, this entailed the hair being long on the sides and with a parting in the center. Called so because it looked as if a bowl had been placed atop their head and the protruding hair cut off. My hair at that time was a completely uncontrollable mass, strewn accross my small head.

Every day at school we'd all have quarter of a pint of milk. It was encased in a minature milk bottle along with a straw. We'd all group around and have a bottle every day after breaktime had finished. However someone had to deliver the milk around the classrooms, and it was delivered upon a milk float. The milk float was made from a car tyre with a board of wood across the middle, with small rotatable wheels attached to the base. After a few years in school we reached class one (the highest class), which was taught by the headmistress. She taught our class with a super stiff upper lip and an iron fist. She sported spiky grey hair and had a wrinkled face with ice cold blue eyes. She had the temper of a lion with a itchy nose (really bad) The worst thing was that I was scared of her and at that time I wasn't a very good worker and recieved frequent rows over it.

That cold winter morning it was our turn to man the milk float. So we did, pushing it slowly at first until we had reached the last class, which was right down the bottom of a long corridor. With the milk float empty and the wind in my uncontrollable hair we pushed as hard as we could and flew balancing on the milk float down the corridor. And as we passed the last classroom door and sailed into the hall, who should step out into the hallway but the school sentinel Ms Thomas herself. We were in for it from that moment on. After our first lashing of fiery fury from her square jaw, we were then instructed to wait outside her office.

It was frighteningly quiet in the corridor, cold also. I could hear happy voices coming from the classrooms. We sat in silence on the seats which lined the wall, they were much too big for us and as we sat in wait for our second verbal hiding Alex began to talk.

"I heard she's really bad, In fact I've heard we might get expelled for this."

He continued to tell me about the unspeakable things he'd "heared" about Ms Thomas. When she returned, she beckoned us into her office sweating, red and flustered. I was completely paralysed standing rigid on the spot where she placed us as she proceeded to give us a calm and quiet talk about the dangers of joyriding. Then we were sent back to our class. After that I didn't tell my mum, I was too afraid of what she would say, and when she asked how school was today, I answerd: "fine."

Writing to inform, explain, describe

 This type of writing includes, for instance:
♠ autobiographical writing
♠ travel writing.

♠ Use the questions below to evaluate the example pieces of Open Writing on PCMs 7 (a and b), 8, 10, and 11 (a and b).
♠ Also judge your own pieces of Open Writing (based on the tasks on PCMs 9 and 12) against these questions.

1. Are the events being described in a chronological order?
2. Have the main events been highlighted successfully?
3. Have imagery or comparisons been used effectively?
4. Is descriptive detail used effectively?
5. Are anecdotes used to bring moments of experience to life?
6. Are experiences looked back on thoughtfully?
7. Is the reader made to feel part of the scene?
8. Are character sketches created effectively?
9. Is a changing mood or atmosphere created?
10. Is any humour used in the piece?
11. Is a serious tone created?
12. Are the writer's (or your) feelings about the experience(s) conveyed?

If possible, discuss the above questions with a partner. Evaluate and mark the piece against each question using the scale below:

5   Definitely
4   Largely
3   Partly
2   Occasionally
1   Not at all

Writing to *inform, explain, describe* overlaps with Writing to *explore, imagine, entertain.*

Also refer to PCM 13 for further questions to consider.

Autobiographical writing: student example 1

Connie Watson, from Lancashire, joined a GCSE English evening class for adults. She wrote the following piece for her coursework folder.

MEMORIES OF THE WAR by Connie Watson

(Sitting in the attic, looking at some old photographs... One is a photograph of a soldier...)

Yes, I remember uncle George so vividly. He looked so handsome in his uniform. I remember Auntie Maggie too, crying as she held a piece of paper, and this photograph in her hand. My cousin Raymond was sat on her knee, and she was telling him that his Daddy was in heaven now.

I was 6 years old, and the war had only started a few months ago. I still remember the warnings we had telling us that the bombs were about to drop. That mournful wail of the sirens would send chills down my spine. A few minutes later the familiar thud as the bombs dropped would scare me to death. Sometimes they'd be nearer and our house would tremble. It was times like that when we didn't have to run to the air-raid shelter. My mum, dad and me would shelter under the kitchen table instead. We soon learned that we hadn't a second to waste, and we'd run as fast as we could. Once inside the underground shelter my best friend Janet and I couldn't stop giggling, when we had to practise putting on our gas masks as fast as we could. I was always glad it was only a rehearsal and we didn't have to keep them on for long. I found the rubbery odour induced a feeling of claustrophobia. We soon forgot our fears, the neighbours would make sure of that. They would tell us children stories and we would have a sing-song. I would do my party piece, and would sing and dance to 'She's a Lassy from Lancashire' with my gran's shawl and wearing my own clogs. My gran would sit there knitting her never-ending scarf. It was the only time I ever saw her with her hair hanging straight down, almost touching her waist. Normally she'd have tied it neatly on top of her head. What could anyone expect? We were still in our nightwear.

The following morning my friend Janet and I would collect shrapnel. We didn't know what it was. We knew it was something special though, because the older boys would swap their best marbles for it. It made us feel important for being up first to collect this special metal, which reminds me... marbles, whip and top, bat and ball and hop-scotch were our most popular games.

I'd always look forward to bonfire day. There were no fireworks or anything else. Everyone was poor because of the war, and its rationing of food, clothes and almost everything else. The poverty never seemed to dampen their spirits on bonfire day. People seemed to enjoy so much with so little. The whole street would come out and sit on their stools outside their back yards, in the cobbled back entry. Every time I watch Coronation Street

Open Writing

it always brings those memories back. We'd have a massive bonfire on the spare ground where the houses opposite used to be. All the grown ups would cook potatoes on the fire. Then we'd have games and a singalong, while someone played the mouth organ.

In those days women would be gone for hours doing their shopping, for there would be queues for food, clothes and almost everything. People would in general only lock their doors on going to bed, they would go out and know it was safe if they hadn't locked their back doors.

What fascinated me most as I grew older was watching aunties paint their legs with gravy browning, then when they were dry, draw a black line down the back of them to make a seam. Only those who went out with yanks would have neat stockings. My gran would warn my aunts about those Americans. 'You keep to your leg tan, no yanks coming here,' she would say. 'There's our Maggie's poor husband given his life, and them lot are trying to take his wife.' Gran was really upset that day because she'd found out auntie Maggie was going out with an American. She told her 'Your George would turn in his grave if he knew what you were up to'. About a year later gran must have changed her mind about this yank, for I was told I must now call him uncle John. I remember her saying to my mum 'He's very good with our Raymond, isn't he? He treats him as if he was his own son.'

Later on I was evacuated down south to stay with my auntie and uncle. I was one of the lucky ones. Most children who were evacuated had to stay with complete strangers. I couldn't see at the time how distressing it must have been for my parents for I was an only child, but they had no choice. I don't remember missing them, which makes me feel guilty now, for they must have missed me. It was so exciting for me living with my three cousins. I was next to the eldest, so me and my cousin Florence would enjoy looking after the two youngest. It was lovely mothering, and bossing them about as well, to be honest. Florence and I became very close. I enjoyed it there so much that I didn't want to come home.

I remember thinking I had seen a ghost when, on returning home after two years, uncle George met me at the station. He was limping and had a patch over his eye. Although he looked a lot older to me, he was still as handsome as ever. I never did find out what happened to uncle John.

It's only now when I look back, do I realize just how poor we were, and what a struggle my parents must have had. At the time I thought that was how everyone lived.

Those war years, they were the happiest years of my life. Being a child at the time, and not knowing the dangers, they were the most exciting years too.

Autobiographical writing: student example 2

Tywi Roberts, aged 16, wrote a full autobiography during his GCSE English course. The extract below was his first chapter and the piece that he finally put in his coursework folder.

EARLY MEMORIES by Tywi Roberts

As you stepped slowly through the Victorian doorway, the room opened up before you. Look up, and view the lime green ceiling looming miles above your head. The windows towered there, giving the room a church-like ambience. Yet, in spite of this, the place still achieved quite a warm and lovely atmosphere. It looked terrifying, but the pleasant people who dwelled there made it happy. Mrs Cardine was the teacher who ruled here with a feather finger. She was obviously a mother, as she had that maternal instinct towards us that only parents have. She was a woman of average height with then shoulder-length hair that was jet black. Whether she wore it at home or not was a mystery to everyone, but she always seemed to be dressed in a dazzling white blouse, which contrasted well with night-sky coloured hair. I never found out as it never really mattered to me at the time, but I believe she was about forty. She was also slightly plump.

We were taught the very basics: spelling, adding, etc. I also vaguely remember being taught knitting at one point. However, on this particular occasion we could make use of the class's wide range of toys. Of course, being a HUGE Thomas the Tank Engine fan (I had all of the dye-cast models), I had to lay my hands on the wooden railway track. This was a tremendous invention, why do they not make toys like that anymore? Basically, it was just several pieces of light wood which could be slotted together easily. They also had grooves cut in them so that the accompanying trains could journey along effectively. Anyway, I had poured my little heart into constructing a fabulous railway that utilized all of the pieces. I was almost finished, and was just laying down the final section of track when I heard the barely audible sound of little wooden wheels on the move. I looked up to see pure horror. A small blonde boy was using the trains on MY track. How dare he! I had built this track with sweat and tears and he uses it for his own amusement! I drew up to my full height and stormed down the line to the source of the disturbance.

'Get away from my track'! I growled aggressively. He turned his tiny golden head and closed the argument with a simple 'No.' That was it. I had tried reasoning with him. Suddenly, my anger was raised to another level. Not only was he using my track, he had now started to demolish it. Words cannot describe the fury that built up within me at that second. I then unleashed it in the form of a soaring fist, which struck him directly in the jaw. The balance that he had obtained in his crouch position was suddenly lost and he fell sideways, right into my marvellous construction, breaking it up into a deformed mess. He curled up on the hard wooden floor twitching. He was screaming as tears flowed from his eyes and down his scarlet cheeks.

My pride in the justice I had administered was short-lived as I felt the powerful tone of Mrs Cardine's Welsh accent knocking me sideways. Her yell echoed around the huge, musty church hall of a classroom...

Autobiographical writing

 Autobiography means writing about your own life. This could be the whole of your life, or one or more memorable episodes. Autobiographical writing is written in the first-person singular – 'I'.

 Complete a piece of autobiographical writing based on one of the following ideas:
1. early childhood
2. outdoor experiences
3. school memories
4. family ties.

♣ Write your piece in the first person ('I'). This is a story about yourself from your own point of view.
♣ An autobiographical story should be based on real events that have happened to you. However, you can use fictional techniques, including exaggeration, to bring events to life.
♣ Include your thoughts and feelings about the events that you describe.
♣ Use descriptive language to add detail and colour to the scene.
♣ You could reflect with the benefit of hindsight on the events that you describe.
♣ Help the process of remembering by looking at photographs and also making notes and lists of relevant people and places, etc.
♣ Your completed piece of writing (for assessment) should be between 500 and 1000 words in length.

TECHNIQUES FOR WRITING AN AUTOBIOGRAPHICAL PIECE

Aim to write a piece that brings to life your personal experience(s) for an interested reader.

♣ Use spelling, punctuation, and grammar accurately.
♣ Use an interesting range of sentences.
♣ Pay particular attention to the opening and ending of the piece.
♣ Think about plot, mood, setting, atmosphere, and characterization.
♣ Include lively dialogue and descriptive detail.

Travel writing: student example 1

Tywi Roberts, aged 16, wrote this description of a school trip to France for his GCSE English coursework folder.

AN ALTERNATIVE GUIDE TO PARIS by Tywi Roberts

The journey through the heart of the continent was extremely wonderful. Three hours on this irritatingly uncomfortable coach with nothing to keep us busy except stare at the autoroute or the nondescript French countryside. Basically, any area of the country that isn't urban consists just of vast fields with no buildings except farms or the odd service station for miles. Even the ground lacks features as there are no hills or valleys either. Some may find it attractive, but I just see it as considerably dull.

The highlight of our journey was simply our stop at a service station. If you saw a photo of their café, you would have no reason to think that it wasn't actually a British establishment. It was just like any fast food restaurant in Cardiff or London or wherever. Upon reaching the counter, I made my best effort to politely request a chocolate muffin. 'Je voudrais...une muffin...chocolat, si vous plaît'. After making more than a pig's ear of asking for my desire the lady behind counter, a large seemingly humourless forty-or-so years old, acknowledged my mumbling with a barely detectable nod. I stood aside to wait for my order, then grinned at my friend's request of 'One chocolate muffin please', before kicking myself upon hearing the response, 'Comin' up, love'.

Upon arriving at our hotel and exiting the coach, I glanced around to see that we were, in fact, in the middle of nowhere. Paris itself was supposedly only a short car journey away, but all I could see was more yellow fields and farmhouses. I turned around to view the hotel itself, a rather inelegant construction, quite reminiscent of the standard English block of flats. I sighed as my gaze turned to the obviously more wallet-emptying section of the building. The well varnished, oaken hue of the dining hall floor and table shone through the French windows, overlooking the Mediterranean swimming pool.

We entered the lobby to view a complex, glowing hub of activity. It seemed that in whatever direction you looked there was a large golden candelabra or gargantuan chandelier, which seemed to beg attention. The layout of the room is what made it complex as there were no 'dormant' areas as such. In the eastern corner, there stood a large winding staircase, underneath which there was a small lounge area with various leaflet stands hanging over the 'loungers'. The sunken centre of the lobby, which seemed like a wide canal leading up to the main desk, always seemed to have five or more people pointlessly meandering from side to side within it, either looking in their wallets or ferreting though their bags as they went. Few were French.

After unpacking in our bland dormitory, we were greeted by the hotel's 'continental lunch'. This consisted of chicken and chips followed by a Cornetto with a drink of coca cola too. Also, the following morning we were greeted by their 'continental breakfast', i.e. baguettes and jam with a glass of orange juice. Would we ever be able to adapt to the French's strange customs?

Travel writing: student example 2

Gareth Pratt introduces his own piece:

'This is basically a true account of four lads and their attempts to climb the highest peak in South Wales. However, some bits have been doctored to make it seem a bit more macho, heroic and generally impressive than it actually was!'

FOUR TO THE SUMMIT by Gareth Pratt

...We struck out at about 6.40pm across Neuadd Dam, through a field before beginning the ascent of Craig Ddu ridge. The ground underfoot was covered in several inches of fresh snow and icy streams traversed our path. Occasionally I rubbed snow across my face in an effort to cool down. The ground then began to rise sharply and the snow began to get a lot thicker. Then disaster struck, I slipped, emitted a strangled cry of 'Aaarrrgh' and crashed into the snow.

'Are you OK, Ga?' Chris yelled.

'Yerrss,' silence.

Then 'Aarrrgghh!' Chris arrived next to me and I struggled to my feet before trying to get going again.

'Listen,' said Chris, 'walk in my footsteps, it'll give you more grip.'

I did as he suggested.

'How's it going, Ga!'

'Fine, really...aarrrgghh!'

I cleared my mouth of snow. 'My wellies haven't got grips!'

We were climbing up very steeply now and I was trying to stay on my feet. Nathan and Hugh eventually came into sight at the top of the climb and I scrambled the final few feet to meet them. We switched on our torches to check our position, but this didn't help much, since the glare reflected off the snow, limited our vision. In the gloom, we could see Craig Fan Ddu stretch away in front of us. Stage two beckoned.

We set off along Craig Fan Ddu towards Corn-Du and Pen-y-Fan, regaling ourselves with choruses of 'Bright Side of Life' as we walked. The wind was hammering across the ridge from left to right, blowing over the cliff. It made walking tough and speaking virtually impossible. Walking was further slowed by the uneven spread of the snow. In places it was only an inch or so thick, yet in other areas, a well-placed boot would sink a good two feet down. After about an hour we decided to stop for a rest and a drink. Ducking down under a ledge of frozen earth, we sat on the snow and listened as the wind screamed around us. It was due to dire visibility caused by a dense mist that we could only speculate on where the edges of the ridge were. After a break of a few minutes, we began to press on, visibility down to a few yards, our world consisting of white snow, impenetrable mist and banshee type wind. I soon lost all track of time and presence. We jumped off ledges of earth into mounds of fresh snow, then scrambled back up one or two feet onto another ledge.

Open Writing

Eventually, we reached about half way along the ridge, where Craig Fan Ddu becomes Craig Gwaun Taf. It is also here that the ridges narrow to a width of about 20-30 feet, with a 900 feet sheer drop on one side and an equally impressive fall on the other side. The sheer drop was on our right and the wind was blasting from left to right across the ridge. At this point walking became slower and it was vital that the ground was checked to ensure a safe footplace could be found. I did not relish the thought of falling and being blown 20 feet to my right before falling 900 feet down. As I contemplated this thought, fear lanced through my body.

The end of Craig Gwaun Taf came into sight and after a yelled conference we decided to by-pass Corn-Du and head straight for Pen-y-Fan. Keeping our eyes peeled for the path that would take us straight to the highest peak in South Wales, we began to walk. We soon found the path and headed under Corn-Du. On one side a white, blanketed slope rose sharply up, while on the other side (right) of us it fell sharply away into the black void. Every time any of us took a step it would send chunks of snow bounding and skittering away into the dark, I shuddered at the prospect of joining them and kept my eyes firmly locked on the path in front. We made progress and arrived at Pen-y-Fan. With the narrowness of Craig Fan Ddu behind us I thought the worst was over, I was wrong in a big way...

Travel writing

Travel writing is writing about a journey or a place. It is often about locations that are unfamiliar to the writer, whose personality may well also be a feature of the writing

Complete a piece of travel writing based on an interesting place you have visited, either abroad or in the United Kingdom.

- ♣ The focus of your writing should be the place you have visited, rather than the relationships within your family, though you can explore reactions to the unfamiliarity of a place.
- ♣ Demonstrate a respect for the place you are describing. Do not resort to unfair, thoughtless criticism based on ignorance of a culture.
- ♣ You can write using the first person 'I', though you can also detach yourself from the scene to be the observant outsider.
- ♣ Include your thoughts and feelings about the place that you describe.
- ♣ Describe the scenery, people and/or situation in detail, so that the reader feels a real sense of place.
- ♣ Do not waste time relating lots of routine details about the journey to your destination.
- ♣ Select and highlight the important incidents and moments of your experience.
- ♣ Your completed piece of writing should be between 500 and 1000 words in length.

TECHNIQUES FOR COMPLETING A PIECE OF TRAVEL WRITING

Aim to create a sense of place with exact observation and authentic detail, including names.

- ♣ Use spelling, punctuation, and grammar accurately.
- ♣ Use an interesting range of sentences.
- ♣ Pay particular attention to the opening and ending of the piece.
- ♣ Think about plot, mood, setting, atmosphere, and characterization.
- ♣ Include lively dialogue and descriptive detail.

Writing to explore, imagine, entertain

 This type of writing includes, for instance:

- writing narrative fiction
- writing a play-script

- Use the questions below to evaluate the example pieces of Open Writing on PCMs 14 (a and b), 15 (a, b, and c), 17 (a and b), and 18 (a, b, and c). These examples have all been written by GCSE students like yourselves.
- Also judge your own pieces of Open Writing (based on the tasks on PCMs 16 and 19) against these questions.

1. Does the opening capture your curiosity?
2. Is the plot developed with interest?
3. Is a complication or twist in the plot used to engage the reader?
4. Does the story build up to a crisis?
5. Is the ending successful?
6. Are characters introduced and described effectively?
7. Is dialogue used effectively?
8. Are the actions of the characters interesting?
9. Are any narrative techniques used, such as addressing the reader directly, withholding information, or flashbacks?
10. Are there any constructive criticisms that could be made about the piece of writing being considered?

If possible, discuss the above questions with a partner. Evaluate and mark the piece against each question, using the scale below:

5   Definitely
4   Largely
3   Partly
2   Occasionally
1   Not at all

Writing to *explore, imagine, entertain* overlaps with Writing to *inform, explain, describe*.

Also refer to PCM 6 for further questions to consider.

WJEC COURSEWORK GUIDE   Open Writing

Narrative fiction: student example 1

Angharad Jones has written a fictional story, but has made it appear more real by using the first person. Although it could be autobiographical, the focus of the narrative is the character Julian, not the first-person narrator.

THE TROUBLE WITH JULIAN by Angharad Jones

Julian was not like the others. Teachers would say he had a problem; his classmates would say that he had a problem. Many concluded that his abnormal behaviour stemmed from an unstable upbringing. They were wrong.

His mother, a kind, plump lady who worked in the local Spar shop, and his father, a refuse collector, had tried their best to control him from an early age; but these attempts were made in vain. When he was a very small child, his mother had expressed a wish to put him into a maximum-security playgroup and his father had surmised that he would become the next Crippin!

In Junior School, at the age of eight, he sported a pair of immensely baggy jeans, which were too big for him, with six inch turn-ups at the bottom, in which he would collect the left-overs from his dinner plate to throw at the girls in the classroom. His favourite ammunition was carrots because, not only would they fly through the air at a great speed, but, when they reached their target (usually the back of a girl's white, crisply ironed blouse), they would leave a radiant orange, mushy stain. The hems of these ammunition-laden jeans would drag on the floor behind him, mowing everything down in their path and dragging it with them.

At one point, his behaviour seemed to be improving, until one Saturday, when he was taken to 'McDonald's' by an aunty who had unwittingly offered to take him out to relieve his poor mother. He had opened his cheese burger and greedily stuffed at least half of it into his mouth, when he let out an ear piercing shriek, followed by cries of 'This cheese is like rubber!' He then ran to the counter, pushing past numerous people on his way, and yelled at the top of his voice, 'I demand to see Ronald McDonald!' until his aunty came and dragged him out of the shop, still screaming.

We were in the same class at school – when he exerted himself and graced us with his presence! He did, however, turn up for the occasional test, at least. I'll never forget the Technology test. I was sat at the back of the examination room, which, as in most cases, was the school gym. Julian was sat in the row to the left of me, in the middle of the hall. As this was a Technology test, there was a trolley with various implements, such as tri-squares and the like, placed in the middle of the room, ready for the second part of the test, which was a practical assessment.

I had just started writing, when I looked up to see Julian slowly pushing the trolley, which was within arm's reach, backwards to the two children who were sat behind him. He motioned with his head, to indicate that he wanted them to do the same. In the space of ten minutes, the trolley had done three full circuits of the hall, unnoticed by Mr Edwards and Mrs Green, who were invigilating. By the time the trolley had reached Julian for the third time everyone sitting in the hall was watching, with smiles on their faces. Everyone with the exception of the two teachers, who were still oblivious to this. Well, until two people reached for the trolley simultaneously and it went hurtling past me, to the back of the hall, and crashed into the wall!...

...His visit yesterday disturbed me. He behaved rather differently, as if he were embarrassed of something. Then, just before he left, he looked at me awkwardly and said, 'Will you go out with me?' and before I had chance to say anything, he sped down the path and out of the gate. It shocked me a bit, so I stood in the open doorway for a while, with a puzzled look on my face. I don't think I'll bother. To go out with him, that is.

Open Writing

Narrative fiction: student example 2

Ruth Wareham introduces her short story:

'The idea came for the short story through a picture that's hanging in my bedroom. It captures the heart of the Amazonian rainforest with animals blending into the background. From this my idea evolved, based on my understanding of missionaries in Africa. It's not really their faith that intrigues me, but the suffering and commitment they had to undergo.'

THE MISSIONARY TRAIL by Ruth Wareham

They pitched their tents on the parched grassy land, their tents in the middle and the two servant boys either side. In front of them was a huge lake whose water was, at best muddy and undrinkable, its colour swirling from the light brown of weak tea to the deeper shades of coffee or chocolate. Pure, cold water was non-existent in central Africa. The blazing sun had drifted down into the horizon slowly that day but now a beautiful sunset covered the sky. Red, orange and yellow blended together like huge brush strokes against which stood the willowy silhouettes of the trees. At night the tents would be surrounded by sticks of fire and a huge campfire. This was all done intentionally to keep wild animals and the biting ants away. The ants were extraordinary creatures, they would march across the forest and jungle in their thousands like platoons of troops. If ever they got into the tent they would swarm the body quickly with their sharp teeth digging into the skin, the pain excruciating. Inside the tents two sticks would hold up a white net to keep mosquitoes and other such insects away. Their two bibles, bound with hard leather, lay beside the couple while they slept.

The Aldworths had been able to carry out their mission with help from the missionary society based at St. Ives. They had begun their journey to the dark and mystifying continent in February 1864 and had been there for over a year. In that time they had built up a strong relationship with savage tribes throughout the jungle. Most of the tribes insisted on presenting one of their finest sheep for 'the white man'. Although their cultural backgrounds were completely different, with many tribes viewing white skin as a superstitious evil, Phillip Aldworth was still able to preach with help from his wife Catherine. Many times the tribes would actually come to believe and know God. They referred to him as 'Muungu Mwenyiezi' meaning God Almighty. Their belief was helped by an unusual incident that also changed the natives' attitude towards these strange 'white people'...

...Into the interminable forests and undulating plateaux of Africa's vast interior Catherine had brought her two young sons, Jacob aged five and John aged three. On the many agonising adventures to the next village, which could only be reached by foot and were sometimes as far away as fifty miles the two angels (as Catherine called them) would happily sit upon the two chairs made

Open Writing

from bamboo while Migogo and Kiboko, the two servant boys, rested the chairs upon their shoulders. The two servant boys were paid for labour…

…In August of 1865 during a season when the temperature reaches well above one hundred degrees and the sun gleams like a ball of fire, water is extremely scarce. That which is found must be strained through cloth and then boiled, which only gets rid of a few impurities. From this, fever and dysentery were very prevalent, even strong men were cut down…

…The party had been walking for at least thirty miles that day and came to a place known as Mukamba. There they camped near a small lake. Their youngest son John got an attack of dysentery and fever. The next day he grew worse, his small round face looked pale and weak. They decided to walk to higher ground, hoping he might recover at a higher altitude. They reached a place called Semguha where they encamped for the night. John's small and defenceless body lay in the tiny cot next to Catherine's bed. She looked over him, tears dripping off her cheeks. Occasionally she would moisten his lips with the muddy water they had preserved. He was in great pain but did not have enough energy to even cry. Catherine drifted to sleep and so did John. During the night she woke up and turned to her son. He looked motionless and she reached for his hand and was terrified to discover how cold his body was. She immediately lifted the child with trembling hands and found her son was dying. He breathed his last breath and his spirit passed away to the God who gave it. Catherine screamed with agonising grief and Phillip stared vacantly in a state of shock…

…Although the loss of their son would remain as an ever-aching grief within their hearts, they carried on with their work. In their eyes everything was in God's hands, He paved the way for their lives. They had decided to walk to a village where a tribe known as Masai lived, at the base of Mount Kenya. It was some fifty miles ahead and considered to be the acme of the danger zone to walking parties passing that way. The Aldworths carried on relentlessly and started the tormenting trail ahead…

…Early in the afternoon Phillip and Migogo went on ahead to find a suitable place for encampment. Catherine and Kiboko were extremely fatigued and found it difficult to keep up with the others' pace. Soon they disappeared into the distance while Catherine, Kiboko and Jacob lagged behind. Catherine took Jacob from Kiboko, exchanging him with the equipment she had been carrying. She started to walk ahead of Kiboko to encourage him to increase his pace. Catherine marched along the track for some time, engrossed with the charming scenery. Suddenly she became fixed to the spot with sheer terror at the sight of a lion and lioness crawling out of the bush before her. The creatures had an aura of superiority their muscular bodies and bulky paws filled the track. The lion's mane shone elegantly in the sun. Catherine's heart pounded frantically, realizing her husband and the two servant boys were out of sight, and there was no one to protect their lives. Jacob squeezed her hand tightly, his bright sparkling eyes transfixed with fear. Catherine mumbled, 'God, if it is your will, save us.' She remembered the policeman's whistle that everyone carried to warn of on-coming danger. She blew a loud blast and to her relief the majestic creatures ceased to approach them, turning instead into a ravine close by and passing out of sight...

...They arose at dawn and after walking ten miles discovered a small village. There were six mud huts built in a semi-circle and a huge smoky fire within its centre. There seemed to be no natives around except for an old lady who sat by the fire. She was engaged in a common practice of smoking a pipe... Catherine tried to get a photograph of the lady... She bluntly refused. Catherine set up the tripod and fixed the camera on top, but the old woman got very distressed. Catherine asked in Higogo (their native language) 'Won't you allow me?' The woman exclaimed, 'That thing will kill me!' Catherine called her husband, who quickly removed the lens cap and took the photo. When Catherine told the old lady it was all done she said, 'I will surely die!'

After walking for a further twenty miles the party broke from the jungle. They now stood on an enormous plain, the land dry and brown. Huge cracks about three inches wide scattered the earth as if searching for water. Phillip was so impressed with the stark contrast between the jungle and the plain that he planted an apple seed to commemorate Africa. This apple might not seem so far away as you might be thinking, as every time you bite into a cape apple you are biting into the history of courage. The four adults and Jacob stared into the distance. They would soon be entering the hazy mirage before them to face the Masai tribe. It was their aim to build a church. So, ever relentless, they lifted their feet and began a new discovery...

Narrative fiction

Narrative fiction is imaginative writing – an invented story, though probably one that makes use of the writer's own experiences. Some stories may be very closely linked to reality, while others attempt to extend well beyond any first-hand experience.

Complete a piece of narrative fiction. It could be based on one of the following ideas:

1. a human characteristic, such as jealousy, ambition, or pride
2. a specialist genre, such as crime, science fiction, or fantasy
3. a quest for something or an escape from something.

- This is an imaginative piece and could be written in the third person, or from the point of view of the narrator (first person).
- Use plenty of descriptive skills to create the setting for your story.
- Develop your characters through both action and dialogue.
- The story should have an arresting opening, a developing plot, a complication, and then a satisfying resolution.
- Plan your story before you begin to write it.
- Your completed piece of writing should be between 500 and 1000 words in length.

TECHNIQUES FOR WRITING NARRATIVE FICTION

Aim to write a story that maintains the interest of a critical reader of fiction.

- Use spelling, punctuation, and grammar accurately.
- Use an interesting range of sentences.
- Pay particular attention to the opening and ending of the piece.
- Think about plot, mood, setting, atmosphere, and characterization.
- Include lively dialogue and descriptive detail.

NOTE:

There should be some evidence of drafting and planning in this task. You should discuss this with your teacher so that he or she can verify that the finished work is your own.

Open Writing

Play-script writing: student example 1

This is the opening scene of a play-script written for GCSE coursework by Elizabeth Evans.

DELIVERY by Elizabeth Evans

A key is heard opening the front door of Jack's apartment. He lives with his best friend, Will. It is Will who is opening the door as he returns home from work. Will closes the door behind him as he enters the apartment. In the middle of the apartment is a very large crate.

Will	(sighs heavily) What a day! Are you in? Jack?
Jack	(from inside the crate) Yes.
Will	What the hell are you doing in that crate?
Jack	It's a long story.
Will	Emily, right? That sister of mine is more trouble than she's worth!
Jack	I don't want to talk about it.
Will	Are you sure?
Jack	Will, I don't want to talk about it!
Will	Okay. Mind if I watch some telly?

Will turns the television on. The patronizing voice of a children's presenter can be heard quietly in the background.

Presenter	...and cut the sticky-backed plastic carefully. You may need to ask an adult...
Jack	Well, if you must know I asked her to marry me.
Will	(turns the television off) (With sudden interest) And what did she say?
Jack	She said she loved me.
Will	That's good, isn't it?
Jack	Then she turned me down.
Will	Oh, that's bad.
Jack	(sarcastic) You think so?
Will	What did she say?
Jack	She said I'm not spontaneous enough. I never live for the moment. That I'm predictable, blah, blah, blah. Do you think I'm predictable?
Will	Yes.
Jack	What!
Will	That's not necessarily a bad thing. It means you're dependable and reliable and...and...(quickly changing the subject) so what else did Emily say?
Jack	She said I don't show her I love her often enough.
Will	You don't?
Jack	Apparently not. I told her I didn't think it mattered because she knew I loved her.
Will	Anything else?
Jack	She said I wasn't spontaneous and I was predictable and not romantic.
Will	You said that. But you're still together?
Jack	Course. You wouldn't believe it. Right in the middle of it all, that silly old woman next door started banging on the wall, complaining about the noise.
Will	Mrs Pritchard?
Jack	That's the one. I don't know why she complains so much. She loves it when Emily and I argue, it gives her something to gossip about.

Will	So what happened then?
Jack	Emily began yelling at her and she banged even louder on the wall. Then once she starts banging on the wall the other one starts on the other side.
Will	Mrs Haversham?
Jack	Yeah. Before I knew it, it wasn't just a row between me and Emily but a row between the four of us.
Will	What was Mrs Haversham shouting about?
Jack	Her nerves. She says arguing is bad for her health.
Will	That's a shame cos she really enjoys it!
Jack	I know! Well, you know how competitive those two old battleaxes are? As soon as Mrs Haversham started shouting, Mrs Pritchard decided to have another go. She was yelling about how the youth of today are so inconsiderate and show no concern for the elderly and infirm.
Will	Infirm! She's probably fitter than I am.
Jack	That's not hard!
Will	Oi!
Jack	(laughs) Sorry. Anyway, Mrs Haversham started telling Emily she should get rid of me because I'm nothing but trouble and before she knows it I'm going to get arrested!
Will	So is that when you left?
Jack	Yes. Just after. (muffled) The whole thing was a nightmare.
Will	What?
Jack	I said, 'It was a nightmare'.
Will	Will you please get out of that crate? I can't talk to you like this.
Jack	Okay. (Jack climbs out of the crate.)
Will	Oh my God! Jack! Why the hell are you naked?
Jack	I just told you. Emily said I wasn't spontaneous enough.
Will	So... you're hiding in a large crate to prove her wrong?
Jack	No. It's part of my plan.
Will	Your... your... Jack, turn around please. I don't want to see you like that! (Jack turns around.)
Jack	Better?
Will	Much. Your plan?
Jack	I'm going to deliver myself to her.
Will	What! You're not serious?
Jack	Deadly. Anyway, I won't be naked.
Will	(sarcastic) Oh, yes. You've got your watch on.
Jack	No, I've got this.
Will	A large red ribbon?
Jack	And a dozen red roses. I'm going to tie the ribbon around me in a huge bow and give her the roses.
Will	(sarcastic) Ooh, mind those thorns!
Jack	Very funny!
Will	Don't you think Emily'll flip when you jump out of the crate?
Jack	No, she'll be delighted that I'm being spontaneous. She'll receive the package and I'll be a complete surprise to her. She'll think I'm wonderful.
Will	She'll think you're crazy.
Jack	She won't. Trust me. It'll be fine...

Open Writing

Play-script writing: student example 2

This is the opening of a radio play-script written for GCSE coursework by Ian Smillie.

SCHOOL REUNION by Ian Smillie

Arch   I say, Bert Root, is that really you. After all these years. You look... um ... um... great!

Bert   You always were a big liar, Archie Jeffries. I look a wreck.

Arch   How's life been treating you, Bert? Not too well by the look of things.

Bert   I've just had a bit of bad luck, that's all. Six months ago my business, 'Bert Root's Canned Vegetables' went into receivership. My house and all my belongings were repossessed. I found myself out on the streets with no home, friends, family or money. Since then I have slept under the flyover in a cardboard box. Two months ago, I got a job as a part-time gardener and I earn enough money to keep me going. I just have to start again that's all.

Arch   I'm very sorry Bert, but I hate to say I told you so. You were getting a bit big for your boots, if you know what I mean?

Bert   You're sorry, huh! You don't know the meaning of the word. We didn't get on twenty years ago and I don't see why that should change for some stupid reunion. So don't pretend to be sorry for anything. Your lies don't wash with me anymore. You've always resented me for my success and I don't expect your attitude will have changed much after twenty years, if at all.

Arch   I see nothing's changed where you are concerned. You're still as bad tempered as ever. As for that matter which I refuse to discuss any further, you should have forgotten all about that by now. It's not healthy to bear grudges over such a trivial matter. Let sleeping dogs lie. Let's not go into all that now. Bert, this is supposed to be a happy event and you'll ruin the evening for everyone.

Bert   (Quietly) Oh, don't worry. I won't spoil the evening for everyone. Just a few.

Arch   What did you...

Rob   Gawd! What's the stench? Who let the tramp in here?

Bert   Lay off, will ya! You'd smell like this if you hadn't washed in weeks.

Arch   Don't tell me! Don't tell me! I know you from somewhere. It's... it's... Robin Conner, isn't it?

Rob   I'm sorry, mate. I don't know you.

Arch   Don't you remember? It's me, Archie. Archie Jeffries.

Rob   Well, I never! Archie Jeffries! I ain't seen you in years. How's it going, mate? Did you know you've got a bad smell following you around?

Arch   That's not a bad smell!

Rob   Coulda fooled me.

Arch   OK, so it is a bad smell! (Laughing) But Bert is underneath it somewhere.

Rob	Bert who?
Arch	Who do you think?
Bert	Excuse me. I do have a voice. I can speak for myself.
Rob	Hang on a minute. I'd recognize that voice anywhere. It's Bert Root, isn't it? Well, well, the great Bert Root – a down and out on the streets of Manchester. I never thought I'd see the day when I was rolling in millions and Bert was a penniless bum. Here's to Bert Root, the most promising student in Manchester University!
Arch	Hear, Hear. Here's to Bert's hard earned success.

(Both laugh and glasses clink)

Rob	Bert, your glass is nearly empty, how about another?
Bert	I can get my own, thankyou. I'm not totally broke!

(Bert walks off)

Arch	Well, someone's in a bad mood. Anyway, enough about that loser. How's life been treating you, Rob?
Rob	Well, as the name suggests, I've been robbing and stealing all the way. Just last month, a couple of the lads and myself drove to Italy in a Fiat Panda. It was dead uncomfortable, but worth it. We pulled off the biggest bank job in history. You must have heard about it.
Arch	You mean it was you? We are not worthy of such great company!
Bert	Did you make it all the way back? Have you still got the money?
Rob	Cor blimey Bert! What's with all these questions? Of course we made it back. We strolled right through customs. Anyway, I wouldn't be here today otherwise. As for the money, I'm living the life of Riley in a mansion in Brazil, right next door to Ronnie Biggs! Of course, it was inevitable that my arrival put his fame into the shade, but we still get on like a house on fire. I risked life and limb to secretly fly over for this reunion. They've got a five-hundred-thousand-pound reward out for anyone assisting in my capture. Great, huh?

(Bert coughs loudly)

Bert	I've suddenly remembered. I've left my hat in the toilet.
Arch	Bert's acting a bit strange.
Rob	What's new? Bert was always acting a bit strange. He is strange!

(Door flies open)

Thom	Wotto chaps! How's it going? I haven't seen you lot in years.
Arch	I... I... don't believe it! Look, it's Thompson Vauxhall. I've seen all your films.
Thom	Why thank you, another loyal fan... Autographs later, please.
Rob	Your only fan!
Thom	Thankyou, Rob. It's good to see you too.
Arch	What are you doing here? I thought you wouldn't have time for such an insignificant gathering.
Thom	I always have time for my fans.
Rob	I'm not your fan! Never have been and never will be.
Arch	Hey, wait till you see Bert Root. You'll get a surprise.

Thom   Oh, no. That arrogant fool isn't here is he? I remember him in university. He was always putting us down because he was so intelligent and sure of success. I used to love bullying him. What use was intelligence to him then? Oh, revenge was so sweet. Hey, remember that time we pinched his clothes and left him hanging from the toilet window by his ankles, absolutely starkers. Oh, how we laughed!

Arch   Here he comes! Look at the state of that!

Thom   What's the matter, Bert? You're looking a bit rough around the edges, hard day at the office? Come to think of it, you're smelling like a pig. What've you been up to?

Bert   You don't need me to tell you my business. I'm sure the other two have managed to fill you in, with delight. Well, I never, if it isn't Thompson Vauxhall. The pompous prat off the TV. I've seen you prancing around on screen like a right twit. I can't believe you actually get paid for that sort of thing. You can't be like that in real life, surely?

Thom   Ooh. Someone got out of the bed on the wrong side this morning, or should I say the cardboard box? Do I detect a touch of jealousy in that comment?

Arch   So, Bert, did you find your hat?
(Pause)

Bert   Um… um… yes, it was here all along. Silly me, eh?

Rob   You're going senile in your old age, Bert.

Bert   At least I'm not going to be spending my old age in Brixton nick!

Play-script writing

A **play-script** might be a full-length play in acts and scenes or it might be a sketch. It might contain a narrator, explaining the development of the action, but most play-scripts are skilfully developed entirely through dialogue, stage directions, and sound effects.

Write a play-script based on one of the following ideas:
1. **two people meet after an absence of at least ten years**
2. **two people meet at an interview as rivals for a job.**

- ♣ Set out your script according to the conventions of published plays.
- ♣ Use stage directions, sound effects, and actions freely. Use the fillers and the punctuation of spoken English.
- ♣ Write no more than three scenes, using no more than three locations.
- ♣ Create two, possibly three, **main** characters, and no more than four characters in total.
- ♣ Aim to give your characters distinctive speech-styles.
- ♣ Develop your characters through both action and dialogue.
- ♣ The story should have an arresting opening, a developing plot, a complication, and then a satisfying resolution.
- ♣ Your completed piece of writing should between 500 and 1000 words in length. This will appear longer than a comparable piece of prose because of the layout of dialogue.

TECHNIQUES FOR COMPLETING A PLAY-SCRIPT

Aim to write a lively play-script that follows the conventions of radio and stage drama.

- ♣ Use spelling, punctuation, and grammar accurately.
- ♣ Use an interesting range of sentences.
- ♣ Pay particular attention to the opening and ending of the piece.
- ♣ Think about plot, mood, setting, atmosphere, and characterization.
- ♣ Include lively dialogue, stage directions, and sound effects.

Closed Writing

Notes for teachers

The English specification
> 2004 and beyond
> Closed Writing 'triplets'

Planning considerations – organizing Closed Writing work
> Links with Closed Writing in Paper 2
> Drafting policy
> Submitting leaflets for Closed Writing coursework
> Monitoring Closed Writing
> Notes on using the photocopy masters (PCMs)

Photocopy masters (PCMs)

GENERAL

PCM 1   Where Closed Writing fits into your course
PCM 2   Making the grade in Closed Writing coursework
PCM 3   Using formal and standard English
PCM 4 (a and b)   Drafting and proofreading
PCM 5 (a and b)   Sample Closed Writing piece (assessment)

TASK SHEETS

PCM 6   Writing to *argue, persuade, advise* – evaluation questions
PCM 7   Report writing: student example
PCM 8   Report writing – task sheet
PCM 9   Formal letter writing: student example
PCM 10   Formal letter writing – task sheet
PCM 11   Writing to *analyse, review, comment* – evaluation questions
PCM 12 (a and b)   Article writing: student example
PCM 13   Article writing – task sheet
PCM 14   Review writing: student example
PCM 15   Review writing – task sheet

Notes for teachers
The English specification

2004 and beyond

For 2004 and beyond, students must have one piece of 'Closed' Writing in their English coursework folders. 'Closed' Writing will take the form of writing **either** to *argue, persuade, advise* **or** to *analyse, review, comment.* Typical work in this section will include reports, letters, speeches, reviews, articles, and leaflets.

Closed Writing 'triplets' of purposes

- *Argue, persuade, advise* – in this section, this triplet is covered through reports and formal letters.
- *Analyse, review, comment* – in this section, this triplet is covered through articles and reviews.

In reality, these triplets will be subsumed and overlapped by the practical demands of a particular task. All tasks will be transactional and/or discursive in nature.

Although the 'essay' is obviously a discursive form of writing, literature-based tasks are not usually successful or appropriate for Closed Writing. Firstly, there is often some confusion in switching from the assessment criteria for English Literature and Reading to those for Writing. Secondly, the balance of coursework and exam practice (in terms of time as well as tasks) is for most candidates already weighted in favour of literature.

Again, literature-generated transactional tasks are valid, but potentially ambiguous in their focus. For example, a social worker's report on Timothy Winters (from the poem of that name by Charles Causley) or a speech from an imaginary trial of George in *Of Mice and Men* are both tasks that might deflect attention from the assessment criteria for Writing.

Planning considerations – organizing Closed Writing work

Coursework pieces should benefit from enlightened teaching approaches to drafting and proofreading. Avoid the open-ended 'project' at all costs – no focus, no sense of purpose and audience, no structure ... no connection at all with the skills and assessment criteria for Closed Writing!

Links with Closed Writing in Paper 2

In the examination, Open Writing coursework links with Paper 1 (Section B), and Closed Writing coursework with Paper 2 (Section B).

Candidates are required to complete two pieces of writing on Paper 2. One will cover the triplet *argue, persuade, advise*; the other will focus on *analyse, review, comment.* Coursework, therefore, should offer regular opportunities to practise Closed Writing skills, rather than a single chance to fill the slot in the folder. One highly successful way of linking coursework to exam preparation is to set an exam-writing task as a timed classroom test, then to require students to develop their response through a drafting

WJEC COURSEWORK GUIDE *Closed Writing*

process into a rather longer and better considered coursework piece.

In this section, each of the four broad task areas has its own relationship to tasks likely to appear in Paper 2, and all four areas require students to have a strong sense of 'audience and purpose'. Generally, too, one would expect a Closed Writing piece to be rather more substantial in coursework than in the examination, though, almost by definition, not as lengthy in most cases as a piece of Open Writing.

Drafting policy

'Clean copies' of students' writing are not allowed in coursework. Students should be guided both during and after the preparation of a first draft of a piece of work, but it is neither acceptable, nor sensible, to correct all errors and then instruct a student to make a clean copy. The final piece should be recognizably the student's own work, reflecting his or her proofreading skills, the honing of which should pay dividends in Paper 1 and Paper 2 when the student obviously has to write independently and under pressure of time.

Whatever the precise details of a department's policy on drafting, it is very important that all colleagues support the policy.

Submitting leaflets for Closed Writing coursework

A task requiring students to write and design a leaflet is recommended for coursework only with caution. There are two reasons for this:
1. the linguistic content of many leaflets is slight;
2. the design and layout features distract students and are given too much of their attention.

Perhaps surprisingly to the lay person, leaflets work well in exams, because candidates have to concentrate on content and language, while dealing pragmatically with the essential details of presentation. In effect, in an exam, students produce the draft of a leaflet. However, in coursework, leaflet tasks too often fail to stretch the best students. With so much material available in shops and libraries, etc. as models, there is sometimes difficulty in identifying the extent of the achievement of the student in producing his or her own leaflet.

Monitoring Closed Writing

It is important that teachers are in control of task-setting and the subsequent process of writing. Where appropriate, students should be encouraged to show an interest in their topic through wider reading, but they should be deterred from copying extracts from resource material of any kind. Any knowledge gleaned from reading should be turned into the student's own understanding through a proper process of thinking and discussion. Closed Writing is arguably best confined to classwork to allow a teacher to monitor the process effectively, particularly the flow of information on the topic being followed.

Notes on using the photocopy masters (PCMs)

PCMs 1-5 provide general information for students, which can be used at an individual teacher's discretion. PCM 1 explains the position of Closed Writing within the English course and PCM 2 explains the grading structure and relevant assessment criteria for students. PCM 3 lists the features of each type of Closed Writing covered in this section, which students should

be aware of. PCM 4 gives students the opportunity to practise editing and proofreading a specimen piece of coursework before they begin work on their own pieces. PCM 5 takes this forward and relates the need for proofreading directly with assessment and grading.

The remainder of this section comprises task-centred work. For each of the four Closed Writing tasks (on PCMs 8, 10, 13, and 15), an exemplar piece of writing has been offered on the preceding PCM as a stimulus for discussion. All of the exemplar pieces have been written by GCSE students and stand, therefore, as realistic models of achievement for candidates across the ability range.

The tasks are not too narrow in focus, but have been chosen so that a wide range of students can engage with them. In other words, there are no specialist topics used, so few students are ruled out of attempting the tasks. Also, they are tasks that a student can do best by bringing his or her own experience to them, not by in-depth research. Thus, the issue of verification starts to be addressed and, to some extent, the issue of time-management in organizing the course is also tackled, for these tasks should not take too long to introduce in the classroom. Please note that with the review-writing task on PCM 15, there is a high potential for students to incorporate derivative review materials here (either from magazines or the Internet). Therefore, the task must be well structured and supervised by the teacher. For the best results, the whole class should watch the performance together and then write reviews on the same material.

On PCMs 6 and 11, there are a number of questions for students to use as they evaluate both the exemplar pieces and their own work arising from the task sheets.

Where Closed Writing fits into your course

Closed Writing is writing to

argue, persuade, advise
or to
analyse, review, comment.

It includes the writing of letters, reports, speeches, and leaflets. It also includes the writing of articles, reviews, factsheets, and newsletters.

You will be assessed on your ability to:

- ♣ communicate clearly
- ♣ use and adapt forms for different readers and purposes
- ♣ organize ideas into sentences, paragraphs, and whole texts
- ♣ use a range of sentence structures effectively
- ♣ use a wide vocabulary
- ♣ use the grammar of standard English
- ♣ use accurate spelling
- ♣ use accurate punctuation
- ♣ present work neatly and clearly

In **English coursework**:

- ♣ **one** piece of Closed Writing will be submitted for final assessment. It will take the form of writing to *argue, persuade, advise* **or** to *analyse, review, comment.*

In **English Paper 2**:

- ♣ there will be **two** transactional/discursive (or Closed) Writing tasks. The first will ask for a piece of writing to *argue, persuade, advise.* The second will ask for a piece of writing to *analyse, review, comment.*

Therefore, be as independent as you can when drafting, editing, and proofreading your coursework, so that you can cope on your own in the examination.

Making the grade in Closed Writing coursework

G > F > E

- Students at grade 'E' can attempt a range of writing styles. There is some awareness of the formats, audiences, and purposes of different types of writing. They can express their opinions and provide some evidence in support. There is some attempt at handling different viewpoints. The subject matter is organized logically.
- They have some control of grammar and generally use vocabulary that is appropriate to tasks. They generally spell common words correctly. There is some control and variety of sentence structures. There is some organization and punctuation control.

E > D > C

- Students at grade 'C' are competent in a range of writing styles. There is a sense of the formats, audiences, and purposes of different types of writing. There is a degree of confidence in expressing opinions, with regular evidence in support. They can handle different viewpoints. The subject matter is coherently and logically organized, and there is some use of devices for particular effects.
- Their grammar is generally appropriate and there is some variety in their vocabulary, which is mostly spelled correctly. They control tenses, agreements, punctuation, and a variety of sentence structures. Their organization is sound.

C > B > A > A*

- Students at grade 'A*' are assured and highly competent in a range of writing styles. There is consistent awareness of the audiences and purposes of different types of writing. They can express their opinions forcefully and provide well-selected evidence in support. They can present different viewpoints clearly and coherently. Complex subject matter is organized and presented coherently. There is effective use of devices for particular effects.
- They can use a wide range of grammar and they have a wide vocabulary, appropriately used, which they spell correctly. They construct complex sentences accurately. They have secure control of tenses, agreements, and connectives. They have secure control of punctuation. Their sentences and paragraphs are coherently linked.

Using formal and standard English

Task

Look closely at an example of one of the following types of Closed Writing that you have completed. Check for the features of that type of writing, as listed below; some of these are interchangeable. All of them require standard English, though some are more formal than others.

Report
- Report heading (e.g. Report on the eating habits of school children)
- The recipient of the report (e.g. To: The Board of Governors)
- The sender of the report (e.g. From: A representative from Catering)
- An introduction
- Sub-headings (e.g. Main course, Dessert, Fruit and vegetables)
- Impersonal style (e.g. avoiding the use of 'I'; for example 'The department has decided...')
- Bullet points
- Conclusions/Recommendations (i.e. suggestions for future action)

Letter
- Your address as the sender in the top right-hand corner
- The receiver's name and address (in the case of formal letters) on the left-hand side
- The correct opening (Dear Sir/Madam, Dear Mr Smith, Dear Editor)
- A suitable and precisely worded opening sentence. Avoid opening with 'I am writing to you...'
- A number of well-developed paragraphs
- A firm summing up of the purpose of the letter
- Avoidance of shortened forms (e.g. I'm, don't, won't, etc.)
- Use of appropriate vocabulary
- Suitable and appropriate signing off (e.g. 'Yours faithfully' – very formal with 'Dear Sir', 'Yours sincerely' – less formal with 'Dear Mr Pit')

Article
- A lively opening containing an idea, example or anecdote that interests the reader
- A clearly argued position on the topic being discussed
- A clear variation in sentence lengths, showing impact in short sentences and subtlety in longer sentences, amidst general clarity
- A consideration of the opposing views
- Integration of supporting evidence and examples
- A conclusion or ending that attempts to take the argument forward

Review
- Stimulate an interest in whatever you are reviewing
- Show respect even if the review is negative
- Steer the reader to your point of view
- Avoid reiterating the plot
- Avoid writing the kind of essay you would write for GCSE English Literature, if doing a book review
- Give the important details, such as key characters' names, venue of performance, etc.
- Aim your review at the intelligent non-expert

Drafting and proofreading

Many pieces of Closed Writing for coursework start life like the piece below by Rachel. Although this piece has potential, it is restricted by its personal and informal style.

Task

1. How could Rachel improve the quality of her report?
   - Think of at least three suggestions you would make to Rachel to help her improve her report.

2. How could Rachel improve her use of language?
   - Work through the text (as Rachel should have done!), adding or changing words and phrases to correct mistakes and make the report more formal and impersonal.

INTRODUCTION

I am submitting a report for the Headteacher and senior members of staff concerning the changes I think should be made to improve the school environment. I hope these changes will be made and that the school will become a nicer place to learn and work for both teachers and students.

THE SCHOOL GROUNDS

I believe rubbish bins should be provided for students to use. There is only one bin in the whole of the playground and this is far too small to cope with all of the rubbish produced by a school full of kids. I think the bins should be placed all around the school and there should be posters pinned up to encourage students to take a pride in the way their school looks.

I also think that any students who misbehave in school or continually break the school rules should be made to pick up all of the litter than lies around the school. This is quite an embarrassing punishment and it should teach them to behave more and to take more pride in the school.

CLASSROOMS AND CORRIDORS

After every lesson, I think teachers should tell the pupils to pick up any rubbish that is on he floor and put it in the bin. Before they leave the class, students should put their chairs under the table and make sure all of the tables are lined up. This should discourage the next class from messing up the room during their lesson. Food and drink should be banned from all classrooms at all times.

I believe the corridors should be kept as free from

WJEC COURSEWORK GUIDE
Closed Writing

litter as possible, otherwise they will become dangerous. They offer a good place to put up loads of posters about keeping the school tidy and litter-free. Bins should be placed in safe places along the corridors to help to keep them clean and tidy. Food and drink should also be banned form the corridors, because any spilled drinks could cause an accident.

TOILETS

I don't think that the toilets should be used as place for students to hang around in. Members of staff should supervise them. Any splashes from the sinks should be mopped up immediately to prevent accidents. I also think there should also be hand-dryers in the toilets to prevent the students from throwing paper towels around and making a mess.

RECOMMENDATIONS

I have four main points that the senior staff members should consider for improving the school environment. Firstly, more litterbins are needed around the school grounds. Secondly, food and drink should be banned from classrooms. Thirdly, corridors should be kept clean and tidy to prevent accidents and finally, hand dryers should be installed in the toilets.

NOTE:

You should seek general help from your teacher in finding and curing weaknesses in your use of language, but you should also get into the habit of proofreading your own work. You need to become a fully independent writer by the time you sit your GCSE exams. If your teacher does correct your coursework in detail, he or she must declare this to the Coursework Moderator.

Sample Closed Writing piece (assessment)

Any errors in the following article on bullfighting by Ellie Rae have not been corrected. Ellie's writing displays a lot of high-grade qualities but occasionally the argument becomes less convincing and is not sustained successfully throughout the article. The final mark or grade would be compromised by these lapses. It is each student's responsibility to ensure that his or her argument is clear and that alternative viewpoints are considered.

Read this piece through and identify all the weaknesses that need to be addressed by the writer.

> Bullfighting, an ancient tradition still present nowadays, has always raised arguments as to whether it should be allowed to take place in the modern times.
>
> Bullfighting originates from the days of the Moors and Christians and has been practised since medieval days (711 AD); an exciting medieval hunt turned into a graceful art. As human beings, we have no reason to be disapproving towards this. The human race is slowly destroying its history and instead of criticising bullfights, we should embrace the fact that this tradition is still going after so many years.
>
> Spain, the country to which bullfighting is immediately associated, even though practised in many others, owes its charisma and heritage to bullfighting. Spain's landscape, architecture. Gastronomy, music and dance would never be the same without bullfighting. These qualities are extremely attractive to foreigners who come an visit, but then they go back to their own countries and protest against bullfighting; Spain's landscape is the way it is due to bullfighting; the openness of the Spanish people is in some way related to the respect for the culture. A mystic writer, Fray Luis de Leon once said, 'The bullfights are in the blood of the Spanish people and they cannot be stopped without facing grave consequences'; words that boast an incredible truth.
>
> The anti-bullfighting groups do have some valid points in their arguments, but are their points really as bad as they seem? Yes, bulls are speared to death and they lose a lot of blood, but a bull, as an animal would have a cruel life anyway, suffering an early death to go to the butchers. Maybe it would be understandable to see bullfighting as cruel if bulls were killed and then thrown away, but they are not. They live an extremely healthy life

out in pastures until the day of the bullfight. Then they stand face to face with a matador, their enemy. They have a chance to fight back. The bulls are then cleanly and quickly killed by the matador. Once dead, bulls get sold to the local market and their meat is used.

Another reason the anti-bullfighting groups say bullfighting is unfair is because they say that bullfights are rigged. They say that substances are put into bull's eyes so that the bull's vision deteriorates making the bulls unable to see the matador. This happens to be most unlikely because the consequences of the bull not being able to see would be life threatening towards the matador. History has it that a famous matador, Manolete died a tragic death while bullfighting because the bull was later found to have naturally bad eye sight, so it confused the red cape with the matador, bursting an artery and sending him to his death.

The final argument against bullfighting is that the horses are blindfolded and are constantly being killed or seriously wounded by the bulls. This is untrue. The horses wear blinkers so that the crowd does not distract them. They also wear heavily padded armour to protect them from the bull's horns. The horses are specially bred and of a sturdy, strong and powerful build. It is very rare that horses get injured let alone die at a bullfight.

In conclusion, bullfighting is a skilful art, a tradition, a part of Spain. Without bullfighting, Spain would not be Spain as it is today and as northern Europeans we have no right to criticise and doubt what we do not understand.

Writing to argue, persuade, advise

This type of writing includes, for instance:
* a report
* a formal letter.

* Use the questions below to evaluate the example pieces of Closed Writing on PCMs 7 and 9.
* Also judge your own pieces of Closed Writing (based on the tasks on PCMs 8 and 10) against these questions.

1. Has the point of view of the writer been expressed?
2. Have different methods been used to support the writer's point of view?
3. Is the writer's case presented persuasively?
4. Is evidence used selectively?
5. Have repetition, reinforcement, exaggeration, or rhetorical questions been used?
6. Has the writer adopted an impersonal style?
7. Is the close attention of the reader gained and maintained?
8. Is the writer's argument logical and clear to the reader?
9. Have the responses and objections of the reader been anticipated?
10. Are the responses of the reader influenced by the writer?
11. Is a counter-argument presented to the main view expressed by the writer?
12. Has advice to the reader been included?

If possible, discuss the above questions with a partner. Evaluate and mark the piece against each question using the scale below:

5 Definitely
4 Largely
3 Partly
2 Occasionally
1 Not at all

Writing to *argue, persuade, advise* overlaps with Writing to *analyse, review, comment*.

Also refer to PCM 11 for further questions to consider.

WJEC COURSEWORK GUIDE Closed Writing

Report writing: student example

Report to the Government think-tank for education

From Alison Thomas (an upper school student in a state secondary school)

INTRODUCTION

As part of a group of nominated Year 11 students, I am submitting a report on secondary education, with a view to making recommendations to the Government. This report will try to present these views clearly and without prejudice, and will make a contribution to this country's education in the twenty-first century.

LESSON STRUCTURE

Some people believe lessons should have a set structure with no room for alteration; lessons should have a structured feel and pupils work better with this. A structured lesson does not have to be one where everyone sits in rows facing the front listening to the teacher talk and then has to work in silence, a lesson can still be structured even if it does not appear so at first glance. For example, at the start of a lesson a few brief guidelines could be given and then tasks could be completed in groups.

Discussion and group work is an important part of school lessons because we learn to understand and relate to other people's views even if we do not agree with them. Also we can learn organisational skills and how to deal with other people and their opinions. They are also beneficial to gain experience in adapting to whatever various situations involve.

TECHNOLOGICAL ADVANCEMENT

Information technology is important in schools even though some pupils are not yet computer-minded. With technology becoming an increasingly more important factor in business, children should be taught how to use various word processing, spreadsheet and database programmes along with other useful software. More and more businesses are using computers and technology in several areas of their work and it is important that pupils have at least a basic understanding of different makes and types of computers.

Every child should be given compulsory information studies and keyboard skills lessons between the ages of eleven and sixteen…

…PRACTICAL ACTIVITIES

Practical activities are important to the education of teenagers, in some cases equally as important as academic subjects. Activities such as netball, tennis, badminton and other sports are good for pupils as they not only help them to keep fit, but can also help them to vent their anger and frustration in a non-abusive manner. Other practical activities such as art can encourage creative tendencies and introduce relevant historical figures in a stimulating way as part of the curriculum.

First aid should be included as a practical subject and pupils should be taught basic first aid, how to deal with accidents and more importantly how to avoid them. Incorporated in this subject could be topics such as safety in the home and how to live a healthier lifestyle. A subject such as this would benefit pupils by giving them vital life skills.

RECOMMENDATIONS

In summary, here are the four main recommendations for the Government to consider:

- Every pupil should have a laptop computer for use at home and in school
- Class sizes should be smaller – no more than 15 pupils per teacher
- Adults should be permitted to join classes and schools should be open in the evening
- Classes should be organized by ability rather than age, meaning that exceptional pupils can be moved further up the school.

Report writing

Reports are written in an impersonal style. They may be written by an individual but they often represent the viewpoints of a number of people. Reports are directed at an official leader of an organization; for instance, the chairperson of a governing body.

Complete the following Closed Writing task:
As a representative of your age group, you have been asked to write a report for the UK Tourist Board. In this report you will suggest ways in which young people could be persuaded to take their summer holidays in the United Kingdom rather than abroad.

- You could discuss the following issues:
  1. the weather
  2. the increase in both indoor and outdoor activities and facilities
  3. the cost
  4. the nightlife
  5. the variety of types of places (e.g. cities, beaches, moors)
  6. access to rail and road transport networks
  7. any other issues you can think of.
- Write your report in a formal and impersonal style. Your target audience is not the young people themselves, but the officials at the UK Tourist Board.
- Use standard English when writing your report.
- The report should be at least 500 words in length.

TECHNIQUES FOR WRITING A REPORT

Aim to use the third-person style (i.e. impersonal style), avoiding the first person, 'I'.

- Use spelling, punctuation, and grammar accurately.
- Use an interesting range of sentences.
- Pay particular attention to the opening and ending of the report.
- Use bullet points to highlight features of the report.
- Use sub-headings to divide the report into clear sections.
- Write a conclusion and/or a set of recommendations (suggestions for the future) at the end of the report.

Formal letter writing: student example

Year 10
Any High School
Main Road
Bedwas
Caerphilly
AN1 0NE

Monday 15th June

Chief Editor
Welsh Herald
Church Street
Old Town
OTT 123

Dear Editor

I am disgusted by the council's decision to close local facilities for two days each week in order to save money. These facilities provide entertainment and a communication link for many people in the community, especially the elderly. It will cause residents like myself great inconvenience and I'm sure that many people will agree with me.

The leisure centre is open from seven o'clock in the morning until ten o'clock at night and offers a broad range of activities. These range from swimming and aqua aerobics to squash and martial arts. The centre offers something that appeals to people of all ages and the long opening hours mean that everyone is able to visit, regardless of when they work during the day. The other facilities offered, such as the gym and sauna, appeal to business people, who need to relax after working all day in the nearby city.

The library is an essential aspect of many people's lives. It encourages and improves literacy amongst young children, as well as developing in them an enthusiasm for literature that will stay with them for the rest of their lives. I use the library every day, as do many of my fellow students, and I find it an invaluable source of information to help with my schoolwork.

The museum and art gallery not only provide an interesting form of education for children, but also attract visitors from outside the area. The regular changes to the main exhibition are always of interest to local people, who cannot wait to see what will be shown there next. The hands-on aspect of many of the displays encourages the feeling in young people that learning can be fun.

Surely if the council wishes to save money, they can do so in other ways. I suggest that they deal with their financial problems by keeping the facilities open for longer hours than usual and focus on advertising the available facilities not only to local people but also to people from other areas. This will result in more money from both visitors and regular users. Instead of punishing the community for their lack of resources, the council should be grateful for our regular use of the facilities and should exploit this in order to gain more money.

Yours sincerely

Bethan Davies

Bethan Davies

  Closed Writing

Formal letter writing

Formal letter writing is important, even in these days of e-mails and mobile phones. Formal letters are still used in business and letters from readers are still frequently printed in newspapers.

Complete the following Closed Writing task:
You are standing for election to the student council in your school to represent your year group, and have been asked by the head teacher to write an open letter to be published in the school newspaper persuading your fellow students to vote for you. All candidates for election have to be approved by the head teacher.

- ♣ Open the letter with 'Dear fellow student...'.
- ♣ Detail your reasons for wanting to be a part of the student council.
- ♣ Consider your personal qualities relevant to the job of representing your fellow students and what you aim to offer them, should you be elected.
- ♣ Consider both the male and female students in your year group.
- ♣ Consider students of all abilities.
- ♣ Consider several aspects of school life on which you have firm, sensible opinions.
- ♣ Be mature and responsible in your writing – avoid suggesting outrageous changes to the school.
- ♣ Write in standard English.
- ♣ Use a persuasive tone in your writing.
- ♣ The letter should be at least 500 words in length.

TECHNIQUES FOR WRITING A FORMAL LETTER

Aim to write pleasantly and persuasively to win the support of your year group and the approval of your head teacher.

- ♣ Use spelling, punctuation, and grammar accurately.
- ♣ Use an interesting range of sentences.
- ♣ Pay particular attention to the opening and ending of the letter.
- ♣ Divide the letter into paragraphs, focusing on a different point for each.
- ♣ Start and finish the letter appropriately. Add your signature at the end and print your name underneath.

Writing to analyse, review, comment

 This type of writing includes, for instance:

* an article
* a review.

* Use the questions below to evaluate the example pieces of Closed Writing on PCMs 12 and 14.
* Also judge your own pieces of Closed Writing (based on the tasks on PCMs 13 and 15) against these questions.

1. Has a fair and balanced analysis of the findings been given?
2. Have different viewpoints been considered?
3. Have the needs of the reader been taken into account?
4. Has the writer given a personal point of view?
5. Has a range of evidence been integrated to support the writer's judgements and conclusions?
6. Has the writer written reflectively?

If possible, discuss the above questions with a partner. Evaluate and mark the piece against each question using the scale below:

5	Definitely
4	Largely
3	Partly
2	Occasionally
1	Not at all

Writing to *analyse, review, comment* overlaps with Writing to *argue, persuade, advise.*

Also refer to PCM 6 for further questions to consider.

Article writing: student example

WINDFARMS ARE GOOD FOR THE ENVIRONMENT

It seems the ecologically-correct scientists were right all along and that windfarms are good for the environment. Wind has turned the sails of windmills for centuries. Now, modern windfarms harness energy from a renewable source and reduce too the need for nuclear power stations. Despite the initial controversy that always surrounds a new development, a survey conducted by the University of Bangor revealed that there is a low level of opposition once a windfarm is erected and in operation.

One of the main groups opposing windfarms is the Ramblers' Association, a group of conscientious missionaries who are full of hot air. Another is Country Guardians, a suspiciously pro-nuclear group that includes that well-known reactionary Sir Bernard Ingham. The Campaign for Rural Wales, with contradictory interests among its natural supporters, finds a consistent and coherent voice difficult to maintain.

Windfarms provide an efficient form of energy and, despite the fears of the general public, the turbines produce very little noise. Any form of power that uses renewable sources of energy must be more favourable than relying heavily on fossil fuels. Wind energy is clean and efficient, unlike the coal-fired power stations whose yield of pollution is nearly as high as its yield of energy.

Windfarms are advantageous to the socio-economic as well as the natural environment. Wales has the highest unemployment figures for Great Britain, so jobs are welcome. Llandinam is the largest windfarm in Europe; it has not only provided a large number of jobs, but also it is undeniably an interesting tourist attraction.

Most windfarms have between thirty and fifty turbines, considered by experts to be an environmentally acceptable number. Windfarms have been built in some of the most inaccessible areas of Britain (inaccessible to everyone except the tenacious Ramblers' Association), including the desolate Yorkshire Moors. It is difficult to understand how anyone could object to these sites, since there is no sign of civilization for miles in any direction and the sound produced is not loud enough to disturb the native wildlife. The wind turbines are far more aesthetically pleasing than the skeletal pylons that grace our countryside at present; any sensible person would prefer to live within one mile of a windfarm than within forty of a nuclear power plant! Minor disadvantages to relatively local people have to be disregarded.

In the near future technological advances will enable scientists to find many more practical applications of windfarms. But successful developments will only occur with the support of a well-informed public. The average person does not know enough about the advantages or contingencies of wind-powered turbines. The strongest winds are found in the middle of oceans; one day we might see huge windfarms afloat in the mid-Atlantic.

Closed
Writing

If all this sounds a little far-fetched, just consider the possibility that one day it might become a reality. There would be no objections from residents or the Ramblers' Association, and the winds would be strong enough to power the whole of Britain. The possibilities for wind-generated power are limitless and soon the public will begin to realize the benefits of this safest form of energy production.

The government-in-waiting supports the development of wind power, but its policy cannot afford to be a simplistic one. A spokesman for Wales' Labour Party said, 'We are concerned that Wales is being targeted for more than its fair share of windfarms. Currently, the Welsh Office deals with planning applications on an individual basis. We will have a coherent strategy for the development of windpower as a key part of our energy policy.' The public is about to get wind of it.

Elizabeth Evans

Article writing

An article is a piece of writing included in a newspaper or magazine. It is not the headline news, but a discussion of a topical issue, often from a particular point of view.

Complete the following Closed Writing task:
Write a topical newspaper article on the subject of heroes. Who, for you, are the heroes of the new millennium? Discuss what makes a hero and write about two or three people of your own choice, saying why you think they deserve to be called heroes.

- Consider the qualities of a hero that are important.
- Think about the importance of good role models for the young (both male and female).
- Address the different attitudes of teenagers and adults to the subject of heroes and anti-heroes.
- Think about the importance of wealth, fame, and publicity in 'hero-worship'.
- Consider the idea of the unknown (local) hero.
- Discuss the influence of heroes of the past and whether they remain heroes today.
- Write the article in standard English. Use your own words in a lively, semi-formal style to interest both readers of your own age and also much older readers.
- Remember, you are writing an article, not a project. Any research for information should be confined to a confirmation of the occasional small detail that you wish to use and need to check.
- Your article should be at least 500 words in length, but no more than 700 words.

TECHNIQUES FOR WRITING AN ARTICLE

Aim to engage the reader's interest in a discussion of a topical subject.

- Use spelling, punctuation, and grammar accurately.
- Use an interesting range of sentences.
- Pay particular attention to the opening, which should be topical, and the ending of the article.
- Write in a semi-formal journalistic style for adult as well as teenage readers.
- Try to include humour, if appropriate.

Review writing: student example

THE AMBER SPYGLASS – PHILIP PULLMAN

'The Amber Spyglass' is the much-awaited third and final chapter of Philip Pullman's 'Dark Materials' series – a complex and radical revamp of 'Paradise Lost'. Indeed, the name 'Dark Materials' is directly lifted from Milton's work. 'The Amber Spyglass' describes the climax of the adventures of Lyra and Will that began in 'Northern Lights' and continued in 'The Subtle Knife'. Any worries readers might have had that this final instalment would be an anticlimax have proved utterly unfounded. If anything, 'The Amber Spyglass' is even more intense and thrilling than its predecessors – featuring bigger and bolder adventures and a fantastic cast of new characters – including what can only be interpreted as a couple of gay angels – as well as the welcome return of many familiar ones.

The 'Dark Materials' story is part of the fashionable new breed of children's literature that began with J. K. Rowling's 'Harry Potter' series. However, unlike Rowling, Pullman excels not only as a storyteller, but also a writer. Pullman's story is intensely dramatic and the language is both vivid and sensuous. He makes frequent subtle references to literature, myths, and science, and his sophisticated and profound ideas stretch adult intellects and beliefs as well as children's.

For those readers unfamiliar with the 'Dark Materials' series, it is a strong cocktail of legend, tragedy, philosophy, and religion, blended with a broad foundation of quantum physics. Throughout the story, the reader is made aware of Pullman's unwavering belief in free will and scientific theory, and his passionate disapproval of the hypocritical practices of organized religion. Pullman maintains that he is merely telling a story. However, this is clearly not really the case; he claims that 'the only thing that's interesting about fantasy is if you can use it to say something truthful and realistic about human nature', which he does – to powerful effect.

Pullman's story takes place in parallel worlds on a scale to rival Tolkien. He clearly does not underestimate the intelligence of his teenage readers and it is perhaps this very quality that means Pullman also has a broad adult appeal too. Despite the obvious science fiction basis of the story, the characters display real emotions, making the fantastical plot easy to believe.

The main character Lyra is part of a repressed society, where temptation is not viewed as the root of all evil, but a release from the oppressive 'Authority'. It is only in 'The Amber Spyglass', when Lyra embraces knowledge and understanding, that her world is saved. This paradoxical presentation of childhood innocence and the repressive nature of the Church is akin to Blake's portrayal of both of these issues in his 'Songs of Innocence and Experience' and it is no coincidence that he is quoted in the opening of this book. In Pullman's world, 'personal daemons' are not merely metaphors for the failures and inadequacies of the individuals; they are personified by animal-like creatures that accompany the characters.

In a recent speech, Pullman claimed that 'when you say "this book is for children", what you are really saying is, "this book is not for adults". But I don't care who's in my audience – all I care is that there should be as many as possible.' With 'The Amber Spyglass' forming the dramatic conclusion to this story, Pullman has guaranteed that his 'Dark Materials' books appeal to both children and adults alike – ensuring its status as a classic!

Elizabeth Evans

Review writing

Reviews are used to communicate a personal opinion about a programme, film, book or performance, among other things. Although they are written in a formal, journalistic style, the aim of the review is to persuade the reader to adopt the same opinion of the performance, book, etc. as the reviewer.

Complete the following Closed Writing task:
Write a review of a live performance you have watched recently.
    OR
Write a review of a particular television programme that you have watched recently.

♦ Use humour, where necessary, to add depth to your review.
♦ Include your personal opinions, but remember to be polite and show a respect for what you have witnessed.
♦ It is possible to write a review of an event such as a football match, but the review should focus on the programme (i.e. the commentary) not the performance of the players or the referee.
♦ Write your review in an appropriate style.
♦ Your review should be at least 500 words in length but no more than 700 words.

TECHNIQUES FOR WRITING A REVIEW

Aim to include your personal opinions, supported by descriptions of events from the performance or programme, where necessary. However, avoid merely reiterating the plot and/or events.

♦ Use spelling, punctuation, and grammar accurately.
♦ Use an interesting range of sentences.
♦ Pay particular attention to the opening and ending of the review.
♦ Include your overall opinions as well as opinions on specific aspects of the programme or performance.
♦ Towards the end of your review, direct readers as to whether or not they should also watch this programme or performance.